PLASTIC SUCKS!

HOW YOU CAN REDUCE SINGLE-USE PLASTIC AND SAVE OUR PLANET

Dougie Poynter

FEIWEL AND FRIENDS
NEW YORK

A FEIWEL AND FRIENDS BOOK
An imprint of Macmillan Publishing Group, LLC
120 Broadway, New York, NY 10271

Printed in China by RR Donnelley Asia Printing Solutions Ltd.,
Dongguan City, Guangdong Province.
Our books may be purchased in bulk for promotional,
educational, or business use. Please contact your local bookseller or
the Macmillan Corporate and Premium Sales Department at
(800) 221-7945 ext. 5442 or by email at MacmillanSpecialMarkets macmillan.com.

Library of Congress Control Number: 2019933682
ISBN 978-1-250-25620-1 (hardcover) / ISBN 978-1-250-25619-5 (paperback) /
ISBN 978-1-250-25618-8 (ebook)

Book design by Janene Spencer
Feiwel and Friends logo designed by Filomena Tuosto
Originally published in the UK by Pan Macmillan, 2019.
First American edition, 2019
10 9 8 7 6 5 4 3 2 1
mackids.com

Picture Credits: page 4 Shutterstock / 20 & 32 5 Gyres / 26 & 27 Huffington Post /
57 Thomas Wood / 58 Will West / 61 Land Rover / 66 Shutterstock / 88 & 91 Kate Arnell /
111 Naturalist Dara / 112 Emmanuel Lubezki / 130 Blue Ollis / 135 & 137 Scot Baston /
143 & 145 CanO Water / 147 Mother and Tongue / 158 James Robson / 161 WWF /
171 Tom Fletcher / 172 Dougie Poynter / 173 Macmillan Children's Books

THIS BOOK IS DEDICATED TO
Sir David Attenborough.
The most awesome human who has ever lived.

CONTENTS

	Introduction	1
1	History of Plastic—It's Not All Bad	37
2	What's the Problem?	45
3	Let's Do Something About It!	65
4	The Culprit Lineup	115
5	Smells Like Entrepreneurial Spirit	139
6	Be Like the Bees	165
	Meet the Experts	176
	Glossary	182
	About the Author & Acknowledgments	184

OUR BEAUTIFUL BLUE PLANET

HAS BEEN GOING STRONG FOR

OVER 4 BILLION YEARS

(OLDER THAN YOUR GREAT-GRANDMOTHER)

BUT NOW IT DESPERATELY NEEDS OUR HELP.
I TRIED CALLING THE AVENGERS BUT THEY ARE
BUSY SO IT'S UP TO US TO SAVE IT,
AND GUESS WHAT?

WE TOTALLY HAVE THE POWER TO DO IT!

Hi! My name is Dougie.

I'm from the same (I think) awesome blue planet as you: Earth. I've always thought this giant ball of rock and gas was amazing, even when I was a kid. In between jumping around in my bedroom, playing guitar (badly at the time), and skateboarding, I used to find myself glued to the TV watching nature programs, climbing trees, observing ants that were farming aphids in the garden, and breeding lizards (okay, those last two are kinda weird). I guess you could say I'm a HUGE fan of Earth.

And the thing is, Earth is in trouble. You've probably heard all this stuff before, right? I know I have.

If you're like me, then you're often left feeling confused. Why aren't the grown-ups sorting it out? Is it actually true?

CLIMATE CHANGE!

ARGHHHH!!!

THE ICE CAPS
ARE MELTING!

ARGHHHH!!!

DEFORESTATION!

ARGHHHH!!!

How on Earth could I help? I'm just one person out of 7.7 BILLION people on the planet! There is a lot of information flying around out there, especially now with so many different social media platforms, so it's hard to know what's really going on—and some of the info is terrifying!

"If only there was a book that pointed us in a simple and correct direction of CHANGE so we could save the world AND still have time to play football and do cool ninja chops before bed," I hear you say. Well, ladies and gentlegerms, boys and girls, cats and dogs . . . YOU'RE ALREADY READING IT!

Just by being a tad more aware of your surroundings you are helping out in a HUGE way. Somewhere along mankind's very rad evolution we picked up more bad habits than we did trash. Humans are very, very intelligent creatures. We went from inventing the wheel to landing on the moon in just the blink of an eye in Earth's history. If we spill our dinner while eating in front of the TV and make a mess on the living-room floor, we usually take a tiny bit of time to clear it up. We don't want to live in our own trash and make our parents angry, right?

Sometimes we even change our behaviors to prevent that mess happening again — for example, by using a TV dinner tray (best invention since the wheel). If we look at our problems a little like that (Earth being our living room and Mother Nature being

our parents), then it shouldn't be too hard to clean up some of the mess and change our behavior without changing too much of our lifestyle. While I've been writing this book, I've been lucky enough to speak to some REALLY cool people who have told me so much about plastic pollution and what we can do to stop it. I've talked to people who've founded charities and people who have started businesses, as well as bloggers and scientists, who all have the same goal—to help protect the environment. And they all agree that . . .

that's where YOU come in.

YOU CAN MAKE A DIFFERENCE.

SOME COOL THINGS ABOUT THE PLANET AND WHY IT NEEDS OUR HELP

Still with me?

Cool. Okay, this book is called *Plastic Sucks!* but before we go into that trash — get the joke? — let's get into the right frame of mind. Try this. I would like you to take a second to think about our planet.

Imagine the lush, green rainforests and the amazing range of wildlife living in them. Giant white waterfalls as tall as skyscrapers. Scorching deserts with huge rolling sand dunes that stretch for miles. The freezing-cold polar ice caps where, even in the coldest place on Earth, life has found a way (I stole that line from *Jurassic Park*) and the gigantic blue oceans that control our climate and where we are still discovering new life. In fact, 80 percent of our oceans are still unmapped!

HOW DO OCEANS CONTROL THE CLIMATE?

Oceans absorb excess heat from the sun. Acting a bit like a conveyor belt, their currents bring warm water and rain from the equator to the North and South Poles, and cold water from the Poles back to the equator. This spreads the heat around the world, keeping hot countries cooler and cold countries warmer.

Now imagine all the nature you encounter at home, either in your garden or on the way to school. Even in the busiest cities and towns, nature can still be seen casually just doing its thing—all you have to do is open your eyes to it. Every living thing on Earth and in the oceans—big and small, from the crawling ant to the leaping antelope—works in delicate balance (I stole that line from *The Lion King*).

Here's an example: Take a deep breath; now take another. Did you know that half of the oxygen on Earth is produced by phytoplankton? What's that, you ask? Well, phytoplankton are tiny single-celled plants found in the ocean that sit way down at the very bottom of the food chain (see next page). Around 50 percent of the oxygen on the planet comes from those little dudes—so that second breath you took is all down to them.

OUR PLANET IS PRETTY AWESOME, RIGHT?

THE AQUATIC
FOODWEB

WHAT ARE PHYTOPLANKTON?

Phytoplankton are plant-like microscopic organisms that live in watery environments, both salty and fresh. As you can see from the diagram on the opposite page, they are really important in the aquatic foodweb, feeding everything from microscopic plankton to enormous whales. Small fish and invertebrates also graze on them, and then those smaller animals are eaten by bigger ones.

Like land plants, phytoplankton have chlorophyll to capture sunlight, and they use photosynthesis to turn it into chemical energy. They consume carbon dioxide and release oxygen. Much of the air we breathe comes from phytoplankton and they are being harmed by plastic blocking out light and tiny plastic particles in the water affecting the food chain. If we want to survive as a human race we need to SAVE THE PHYTOPLANKTON by reducing the plastic in the oceans.

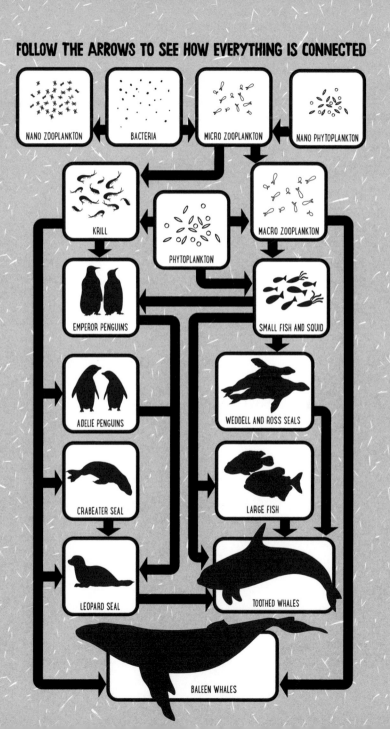

FOLLOW THE ARROWS TO SEE HOW EVERYTHING IS CONNECTED

PLANET EARTH BLOWS MY MIND EVERY DAY.

In my opinion, planet Earth is the best happy accident to ever happen in the universe. Latest studies suggest that water was first on this Earth around 4.6 billion years ago. This, combined with the fact that our sun is the perfect distance away (see opposite), and a mixture of ice ages and volcanic gases (Earth farts) that create chemical reactions, means that somehow life happened.

That's the short version. Okay, that's the very short version. But the planet has gone through some radical changes over the last billions of years for us to be able to climb up out of the water and slowly evolve into the amazing creatures we are today.

WHAT IS THE GOLDILOCKS ZONE?

There are a few key factors that allow a planet to support life. The most important one is the presence of water. This is determined by the planet's distance from its star (so in Earth's case, the sun). If a planet does exist in a star's habitable zone—the Goldilocks Zone—and atmospheric conditions allow for liquid water to be present, then life may form.

Planets that are closer to the sun than us, like Venus, are unable to host life because they're too hot. Liquid water therefore can't exist on these planets. Other planets are too far from the sun, which means they are so cold that only water in the form of ice exists. Or the planet may even be made entirely of gas, like Neptune and Uranus. Earth, fortunately for us, is the perfect Goldilocks distance from the sun: not too far, not too close. Just right.

5 SCARY FACTS
ABOUT OUR PLANET

1 OUR FORESTS ARE UNDER SERIOUS THREAT.

Thirty-one percent of the Earth is covered in life-giving forests. These green areas of the world breathe in the carbon dioxide that we breathe out, and in return they produce the oxygen that we need to survive. So, as you can imagine, the more forests that are cut down, the less oxygen we have. And let's not forget about the amount of animals (more than half the species we know of) that live in these forests and are left without homes whenever we destroy their habitat.

2 ANIMALS AND PLANTS ARE DISAPPEARING AT RECORD RATES.

And it's not just the big ones that are under threat, like tigers and rhinos, but also unseen yet vital insects like dung beetles and earthworms, as well fish and coral reefs in the oceans. That's not just a tragedy in itself, but it can change whole ecosystems. If you don't have lions, for example, then the zebra and gazelle populations explode and they eat all the grass and turn huge parts of Africa into deserts.

3 YOU'VE PROBABLY HEARD THAT THE CLIMATE IS CHANGING AND IS GETTING WARMER ALL THE TIME.

You might think that sounds great because there will be more sunny days, but, in fact, it is leading to big problems like rising sea levels, more droughts and more floods, more disease and more wildfires. It's younger people who are going to feel the worst effects of climate change. That's why thousands of kids around the world have been going on school strike — to tell the grown-ups to hurry up and start sorting it out!

4 THERE'S A REASON WHY EARTH IS KNOWN AS THE BLUE PLANET.

Most of it is water. That water is vital to all life and it's one of the most important reasons that we're here. However, most of it is seawater and not available to us to drink. Only 3 percent of it is fresh water that we can drink, and we're not taking enough care of the water that we *do* have. Most of it goes into growing crops, which is great, but it is often used wastefully so we need to be smarter about how we use it. More than a billion people don't have access to clean water and many cities around the world are running short.

5 OUR AIR IS POLLUTED.

We all take for granted the ability to get around in cars, buses, trains, and planes, as well as the stuff that we use that's produced in factories around the world. But all these machines pump pollution into the atmosphere, and that is bad for our health. It makes it difficult to breathe and causes all sorts of other serious problems too. On top of that, this pollution contributes to climate change and makes it harder to grow food.

So let's recap. The forests that give over 80 percent of our plants and animals their homes are being cut down, at a rate of sixty soccer fields a minute. The forests are cut down to create farmland and more space for people to live in, and for paper and wood. SCARY STUFF, RIGHT? I had heard all that before, too, but there was never really a SOLUTION. It seemed like it was just, "Hey, isn't the planet beautiful? Well, it's being destroyed. Okay, bye."

BUT THERE IS A SOLUTION— STAY WITH ME!

HOW I GOT

INVOLVED...

I spend a lot of my time in Los Angeles (mainly because I'm a wimp and really like warm weather). And while I'm over there I get to meet some really cool people.

NORTH
PACIFIC GYRE

NORTH
ATLANTIC
GYRE

SOUTH
PACIFIC GYRE

SOUTH
ATLANTIC
GYRE

A couple of years ago I was lucky enough to be introduced to two awesome people called Anna Cummins and Marcus Eriksen. These guys are literally the real-life Indiana Jones and Lara Croft. They dig up dinosaurs and know heaps about the ocean.

Anna and Marcus started a charity called 5 Gyres (named after the five major systems of circulating ocean currents), which is dedicated to spreading awareness of plastic pollution in the ocean.

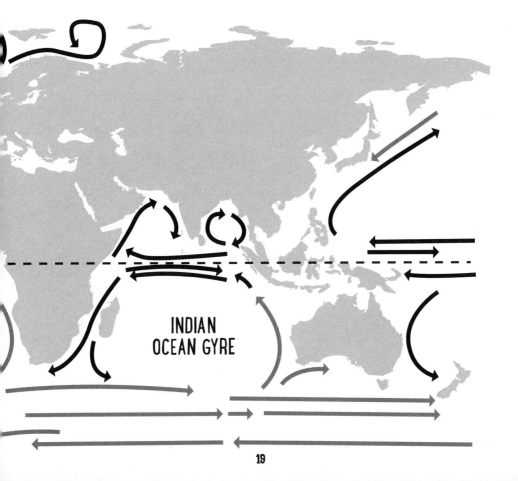

INDIAN
OCEAN GYRE

Marcus is not only incredibly handsome but incredibly brave too. Once he traveled across the Pacific Ocean for three months on a JUNK RAFT made of plastic to raise awareness of how much junk from land was ending up in the oceans! I asked him if he survived . . . I don't think he got it.

Talking to them was the first time I ever heard about microbeads and I was shocked as they told me more.

EXPERT BOX

WHAT ARE MICROBEADS?

Microbeads are teeny tiny pieces of plastic. In the late '90s and early 2000s, they started to replace natural ingredients in lots of toiletries, because they create a silky texture in the product. So things like shampoo, toothpaste, makeup, lotions, face wash, sunscreen, shaving cream, and exfoliators can be full of them!

Each bead is normally smaller than five millimeters, which means that they're small enough to go down your drain—so once you've washed your face or brushed your teeth with them they go down the drain and end up in the ocean (remember how everything leads to the ocean?).

Anna and Marcus explained to me that, aside from all the larger plastics you can see, there are literally billions or trillions of microplastics you can't see. Some are broken-down bits of larger pieces of plastic, but the majority come from normal everyday household stuff like toothpaste, face wash, and body scrubs . . . Yeah—TOOTHPASTE! I guess they were put in there to add a texture so you kind of feel like your teeth were getting extra clean? I'm really not sure, but whatever the reason, it's CRAZY!

All these little beads are going down our drains, and you know what they say in *Finding Nemo*: "All drains lead to the ocean . . ." (man, I have to chill with the quotes). Millions and millions of plastic beads are entering the ocean, because sewage systems can't filter things that tiny, and then these are being eaten by small animals and slowly making their way up the food chain.

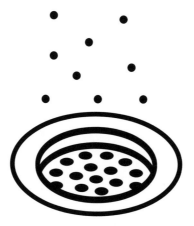

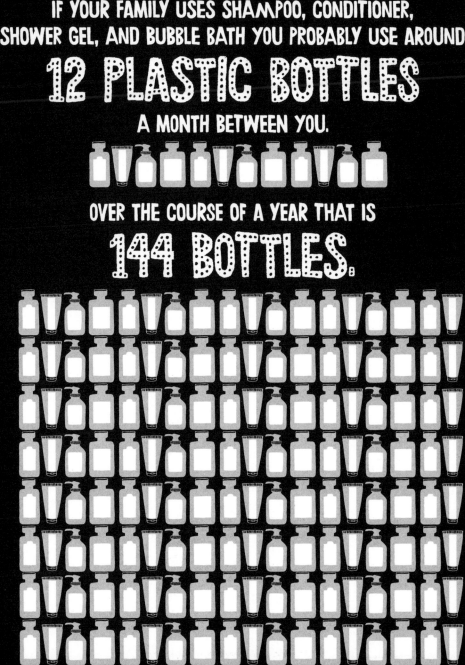

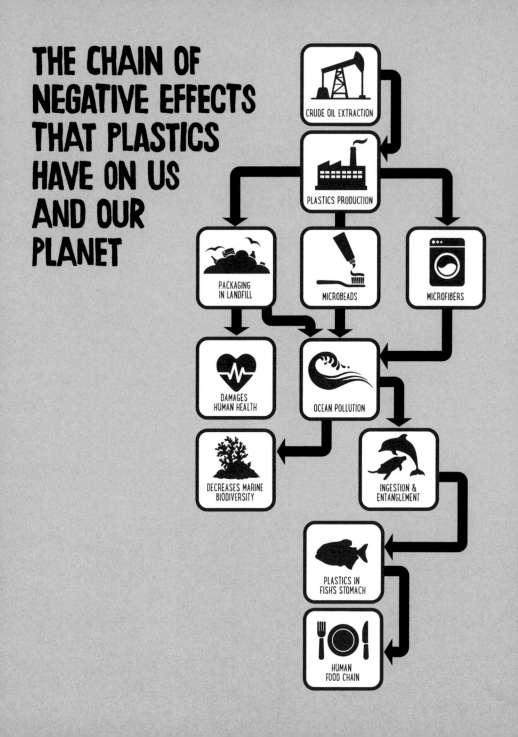

NOW 1 IN 4 FISH CONTAINS PLASTIC . . .

And what sucks even more is plastic absorbs toxins like a sponge, so when fish and other wildlife consume plastic, the toxins can cause digestive problems, malnutrition, and even death. And if humans eat a fish that has been snacking on plastic, some of those toxins can transfer to us. So yeah, the microbeads from your toothpaste could end up in your sushi!

. . . THAT REALLY SUCKS!

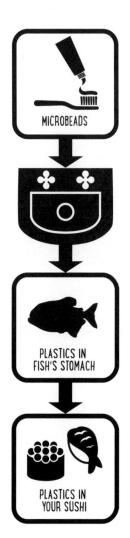

MICROBEADS

PLASTICS IN FISH'S STOMACH

PLASTICS IN YOUR SUSHI

Anna and Marcus have been campaigning against microbeads for years, and back in 2015 they worked with a large coalition of NGOs (non-governmental organizations) to get microbeads banned from personal care products in the US. President Obama signed this law at the end of 2015, and microbead products were banned from the shelves by 2018. This was a huge accomplishment for the environmental movement. Hooray!

But . . . when I got back home I found out that microbeads had not yet been banned in the UK. I knew that I had to do something, but I wasn't sure where to start.

The cynical (or lazy) part of me just thought, *Oh well, I don't really have the power to do anything about this* and *There's probably someone else already on the case,* but for the first time, thankfully, I ignored that voice in my head. For a while I became obsessed with telling everyone I knew about the problem. Then I took it a bit further and started posting information and pictures on social media (in among pictures of me getting some serious air onstage). Not long after I was doing interviews with the

Dougie Poynter
Musician

3k

THE BLOG

Why We Must Stop U.

We have the power to create change and a shift in
has the ability to voice our opinions against this iss
conversation about plastic pollution to our friends,
Every unused bottle matters.

29/06/2016 06:00 BST | **Updated** 29/06/2017 06:12 BST

Guardian newspaper and the *Huffington Post* and having conversations with people in parliament.

The parliament dudes said that although they agreed microbeads sucked, the chances of having a ban put in place were slim. This is because our government is majorly influenced by the oil companies that make plastic. That's the complicated part that really SUCKS. I came home after that day really bummed out and deflated — of course, the people at the top make all the decisions and what can you do when they say no? But, much to my surprise, a few days later I found out that some other people had started a petition to get the beads banned.

Everywhere I looked I saw more and more anti-microbead tweets, Instagram posts, and news articles. People were shocked that they had unwittingly been part of the problem — they wanted to change right away and let as many other people know as possible. Before I knew it I was part of this huge snowball of people wanting to take positive action! Not long after that, I woke up to the news that they were banning the bead in the UK, just like in America. The ban initially barred the manufacturing of products with microbeads in January 2018, then a ban on sales followed in July 2018.

g Microbeads

e. Each of us
d start
and leaders.

Jumping on board with the microbead campaign was one of the most enlightening things I have ever done. One, because I had NO idea how many products I had used in the past that contained them. And two, because I was so humbled by the amount of people that listened and got on board. Usually I'm quite nervous when it comes to talking to newspapers or journalists, but everyone I spoke to from the press wrote great articles using the info that I had given them.

IT ALSO GAVE ME THIS
HUGE SENSE OF FAITH
IN US AS HUMANS.

I was pretty sure that people wouldn't be as interested as me. Turns out humanity can be pretty awesome—the feedback was overwhelming. Every day, I would get messages on social media about other people making changes and also doing what they could to make a difference . . . and, well, that just made me super happy that people care.

After the microbead ban I was pretty stoked in knowing that I had played even just a small part in that campaign.

NO MORE
PLASTIC

I'M NO SCIENTIST, LAWYER, OR ANYTHING ELSE THAT SOUNDS GROWN-UP AND IMPORTANT.

I'm just your average person who has a love for wildlife and the oceans and a natural curiosity and concern about pollution. And that's how this book happened, just from caring and wanting to pass on what I had learned.

SAVE OUR PLANET

BAN THE BEADS

I guess my point is that

I TRULY BELIEVE THAT WE
CAN MAKE A DIFFERENCE
IF WE BELIEVE WE CAN.

One of the most awesome things I have been hearing about lately is youth campaigners. I think our youth is the most important generation for environmental awareness. I mean, you guys are literally the future! Future politicians, doctors, scientists, inventors, artists—future everything. The coolest thing about youth campaigners is seeing how seriously the older generation takes them. There have been countless stories about kids standing up to make a change, and I think it's awesome!

WITH A BIT OF
AWARENESS
AND THE RIGHT
COURSE OF ACTION,
EVEN THE SMALLEST CHANGES
IN OUR EVERYDAY LIVES
ARE HAVING A
HUGE IMPACT.[8]

5 GYRES INTERVIEW

WHO ARE YOU AND WHAT DO YOU DO?

Marcus: We are the 5 Gyres Institute —we study plastic in the world's oceans. We've run about twenty expeditions crossing all oceans, studying plastic pollution in the most remote parts of the planet. We bring that scientific information back to land, publish papers on it, and from there come action plans to try to stop the flow of this trash from land to sea.

Anna: We realized that there was a large gap in the global research. Not being a scientist myself, it had not occurred to me that we could do this on our own, but we did! We have now been able to go to all five gyres —which are those circulating current systems where plastic accumulates —and do the research to show not only that we need global solutions to a global problem, but that we need to start locally.

WHY WASN'T THERE MUCH SCIENTIFIC FOCUS ON THE PLASTIC PROBLEM IN THE OCEAN?

Anna: A couple of things. There has actually been scientific research on ocean plastic dating back to the '70s, but it is only recently that the world has started paying attention. One part of the problem is that scientists aren't always the best communicators. They talk to each other within the scientific community, but it's difficult to translate the information and take it to the public. It takes messengers who can connect the science to everyday life and everyday people, not just to show that it is a problem but to show that people can get involved in the solution.

Marcus: In the last few years there has been this global groundswell—there is an organization called Break Free From Plastic that, very simply, has put a set of values out to the world on ways that we can reduce our plastic use. And over 1,400 organizations from all over the world have come together and said, "Okay, we need to break free from plastic use, especially single-use products and packaging. They are trashing communities worldwide."

Anna: Another thing that Break Free From Plastic and other similar organizations are doing is starting to get producers to take responsibility—so the businesses who are creating the plastic take responsibility for recovering and recycling their products. The brand audit was one tool—around the world people have started to make a note of which brands they are finding on their beach clean-ups and using that information to say, "It is not just about people littering, but about producers making this stuff that doesn't have any value."

Companies have been making single-use plastic bags, straws, and bottles for half a century and not taking responsibility for the full life cycle of the product. There are almost eight billion people on the planet who have a thirst for a better, more convenient lifestyle, but so many of the things they need for this comes packaged in plastic: a material with no end game, except being buried or burned. The world has had enough.

Dougie: That makes me think about big gigs with McFly. If we wanted to use a confetti cannon at the end of the show, it was our responsibility to clean it up afterward. The band has to pay a fee to cover those costs. It makes you think harder about whether you want to use it. If companies had to pay to clean up their packaging after it had left their warehouses, they would think more carefully about what they use, and come up with alternative solutions.

HOW DID YOU GET INVOLVED IN WHAT YOU DO?

Marcus: My experience goes back to being in the first Gulf War in 1991, when the US and UK went to liberate Kuwait after Iraq had invaded. I was one of the marines on the ground among all the burning oil wells, and I remember being covered in little drops of raw petroleum, looking at the burning wells and thinking: *What are we doing here? What are we fighting for?* I learned all about the foreign policy to protect access to petroleum, but it's just not the same as seeing the true cost of war, the cost of fossil fuel. From fossil fuels we don't just get energy, we get chemistry, and almost 99 percent of plastics.

While I was in the desert I made a promise to myself: If I survived, I would raft down the Mississippi. I made good on that promise thirteen years later, on a raft made from plastic bottles. And all along the river I saw trash: bottles, cups, and bags, all heading out to sea. I came back to LA and had the chance to visit the Midway Atoll in the middle of the Pacific. This island is a breeding spot for albatrosses and so, as well as seeing loads of these amazing birds, there were loads of albatross skeletons — and inside every skeleton I could see trash. So at this point I knew the cost of petroleum, I knew the environmental costs and now I saw the impact on marine life. When I came back to LA, I tracked down Captain Charles Moore and asked to see the garbage patch he had found, and from that point I was hooked and on the path to research plastic pollution.

Anna: Captain Charles Moore was my way in, too. In 2001, I heard him give a lecture at a conference. He talked about this area of the Pacific Ocean filling up with trash — plastic specifically — and no one was talking about it then. And the problem just hit me like a thunderbolt! I wanted to know how I could get involved. So I went out to Guadalupe Island in 2004 with Captain Moore, then I met Marcus and we began working together, then we went out to see the gyre.

HOW BAD IS THE PROBLEM? WHAT DID YOU FIND?

Marcus: During our expeditions we found some big stuff — a lot of plastic fishing nets and buoys — but we also found a confetti of small particles of plastic. There were small pieces in the oceans, hanging like a smog over a city, from the surface all the way down to the seafloor, mostly in the gyres, but all over the ocean, really: We have found it in the Arctic, Antarctica, the Bay of Bengal, and in the Great Lakes. These microplastics are in our drinking water, in fish, in shellfish, in our sea salt, and in our honey.

Dougie: That all sounds really worrying.

Anna: I must add that despite how ubiquitous this problem is, we lately have been feeling more hopeful. We could actually turn this thing around.

Marcus: I do feel much more optimistic than I did ten years ago. If we can reduce the amount of trash in our rivers by 20 percent each year, in seven years we would get the environment in better balance.

HOW DO WE DO THAT?

Marcus: How do we turn off the tap? How do we get communities to stop the movement of trash to the sea? It needs to start at a local level. Here's a good example that made a difference and influenced others: We went to a middle school in Los Angeles and told them about the issue, and the kids got the principal to switch from disposable styrofoam lunch trays to reusable. They saved 1,000 trays a day and $12,000. The district commissioner came to see them and was impressed and eventually the whole district—that's 9,000 schools—switched.

Dougie: Another example is how, in the past twelve months, we've seen a massive change in how people view straws in this country. If you get one now it tends to be paper and people feel happy refusing a straw. Straws have become taboo.

Anna: That is great. We need to get to the tipping point where it becomes taboo to have a plastic bag, straw, or bottle.

WHAT IS YOUR TOP TIP?

Anna: Everyone can do something—find an organization you want to support and get involved.

"BECAUSE EACH ONE OF US IS PART OF THE PROBLEM, IT ALSO MEANS THAT EACH ONE OF US CAN BE PART OF THE SOLUTION."

—LYNDSEY DODDS, HEAD OF MARINE POLICY, WWF

1
HISTORY OF PLASTIC
IT'S NOT ALL BAD!

WHERE DID IT COME FROM?

Before we get going on how to reduce the plastic you use and clear up the plastic already out there, let's learn a bit about it. Who invented it? Is it really all bad? How did it go so wrong?

You may have already wondered where this colorful and shape-shifting invention came from, and why. If plastic is so bad for the planet, then why the heck was it invented in the first place? It's a pretty simple story, really, and it isn't just one person's fault for things getting out of hand. Lots of inventors and scientists were involved along the way, inventing and innovating ways for us to lead cleaner and better lives.

In the early days, before 1600 BCE, early Native Americans made rubber from the natural latex of the rubber tree. One of the uses for this rubber was to turn it into balls to be used as sacred offerings in the temples—it was also used for ball games.

Fast forward to...

1839 Vulcanization, the process of adding sulphur to heated rubber, is invented by American Charles Goodyear. This makes the rubber stretchier and more malleable.

Used for tires and shoes ⟶

1856 Alexander Parkes from Birmingham invents an early celluloid (synthetic plastic material) and names it Parkesine. Many early examples of Parkesine products—printers' molds, cutlery handles, buttons, combs—can be found on display at London's Science Museum.

1870 Celluloid further developed by two Americans, the Hyatt brothers, thus providing what would become the raw material used by the film industry to make and record movies.

1907 Bakelite is invented. Named after its Belgian creator, Leo Baekeland, Bakelite is a world-changing synthetic plastic. It is launched in 1909 with the slogan "the material of 1,000 uses" and was used to make the iconic Bakelite phone.

HISTORY OF PLASTIC

 And stretchy nylon tights!

1939 Nylon launches—and in 1969 Neil Armstrong plants a nylon flag on the moon.

1941 PET (polyethylene terephthalate) is first produced.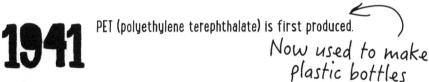

Now used to make plastic bottles

1939-1945 Plastics are in high demand during World War II.

Nylon and Perspex plastic was shaped and molded into everything from cockpits and parachutes to hand grenades.

**1950S** The first polyethylene bags appear.

1960S **ONWARD**: Plastics are further toughened and refined, allowing them to compete with metals.

THE WORD "PLASTIC" COMES FROM THE GREEK WORD PLASTIKOS, WHICH MEANS "CAPABLE OF BEING SHAPED OR MOLDED."

It took a little while for people to realize what they could really do with this new, revolutionary product. It was lightweight, long-lasting, could be shaped into anything, and it came in any color you wanted — the possibilities were endless!

Bike and sports helmets

Bulletproof vests

Phones

TODAY, PLASTIC IS USED IN ALL SORTS OF IMPORTANT WAYS.

Seat belts

Airbags

Car bodies

41

AND THINK ABOUT HOW MUCH PLASTIC HAS CHANGED THINGS FOR MEDICINE AND HOSPITALS.

IN 1982 THE FIRST ARTIFICIAL HEART, MADE MAINLY OF POLYURETHANE, WAS IMPLANTED IN A HUMAN.

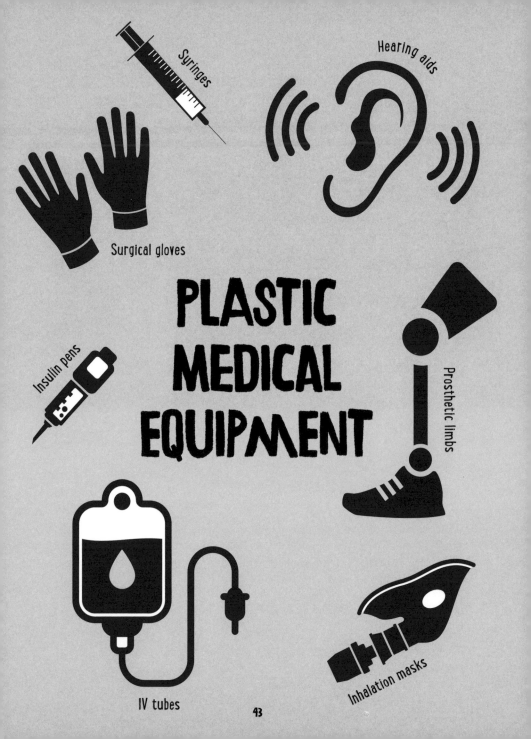

Syringes

Hearing aids

Surgical gloves

PLASTIC MEDICAL EQUIPMENT

Insulin pens

Prosthetic limbs

IV tubes

Inhalation masks

These are all things that are used daily to help improve our lives and sometimes SAVE THEM. Plastic really helps us keep everything safe and clean, which is important to avoid contamination—germs being spread. But, still, hospitals around the world are trying to avoid single-use plastic where they do not feel it is necessary.

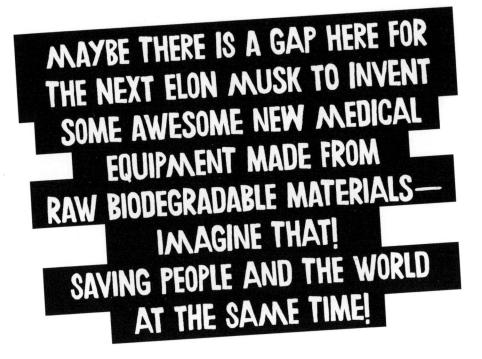

MAYBE THERE IS A GAP HERE FOR THE NEXT ELON MUSK TO INVENT SOME AWESOME NEW MEDICAL EQUIPMENT MADE FROM RAW BIODEGRADABLE MATERIALS— IMAGINE THAT! SAVING PEOPLE AND THE WORLD AT THE SAME TIME!

Over a few decades plastic had gone from being something exclusive to something that is found in every household the world over. Plastic wasn't really a part of daily life and then—BOOM!—it's now in everything from food storage to stockings.

JUST THINK, YOUR LUNCH BOX IS GOING TO LIVE TO BE 400 YEARS OLD!

2

WHAT'S THE PROBLEM?

HOW WE STARTED OVERUSING PLASTIC

The trouble started when plastic went from being a valuable material that helped propel the human race into the future, to something we were overusing and over-producing, without a thought for what would happen when we threw it away. So how did we get to that point?

At the end of World War II the plastic companies switched their attention — and their advertising — over to the general public (us) so that the durable material was being sold as a SINGLE-USE, DISPOSABLE product. (Booooooooo.)

SINGLE-USE PLASTIC

Single-use plastics, or disposable plastics, are used only once before they are thrown away or recycled. These items are things like plastic bags, straws, coffee stirrers, water bottles, and most food packaging.

AT THE START OF THE 1950S A NEW PRODUCT WAS DEVELOPED—

HIGH-DENSITY POLYETHYLENE,

WHICH MEANT THAT PLASTIC BOTTLES WERE CHEAPER TO MANUFACTURE AND BUY. NOW YOU CAN'T GO ANYWHERE WITHOUT SEEING THEM.

RECENT STUDIES SHOW THAT, GLOBALLY, HUMANS BUY

A MILLION PLASTIC BOTTLES PER MINUTE,

THE MAJORITY OF WHICH ARE NOT RECYCLED. IT IS ESTIMATED THAT OVER HALF A TRILLION PLASTIC BOTTLES WILL BE SOLD IN 2020.

RISE IN WORLD PRODUCTION OF PLASTICS

In million tons!

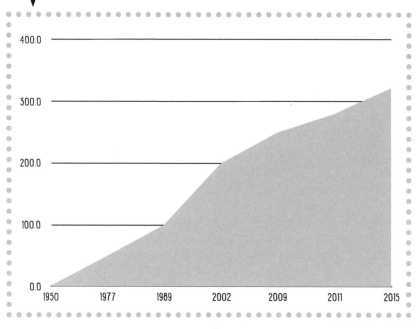

By 1970 (when everyone wore flares), chain coffee shops started to pop up everywhere, selling coffee and hot drinks served in disposable plastic-lined cups and food served with plastic cutlery. The number of coffee shops has ballooned ever since, and with it so has the use of plastic. (A 2018 study showed there were 590 UK coffee shops in 1999 and over 7,470 in 2018.)

SURPRISING PLASTIC

Plastic is now in things like cars, furniture, cosmetics, and electronics. But it's also in a bunch of things you would not necessarily expect.

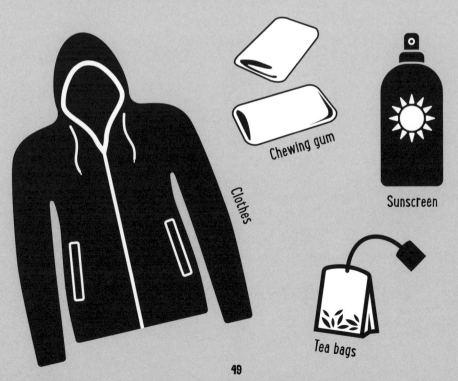

Chewing gum

Clothes

Sunscreen

Tea bags

WHAT'S THE DAMAGE?

This part of the book is probably the biggest bummer. As we've seen, plastic is everywhere and we are all making far too much use of it. We simply didn't know about or understand the damage that our use of plastic was causing. We know now and are willing to refuse plastic and try something new.

So, a HUGE portion of the trash we just throw away ends up in the ocean. This is mainly from water washing it into lakes, streams, and drains, which lead to the ocean. Loads of plastic bags are actually picked up by the wind from landfills and blown miles out into the sea!

Plastic is a substance the Earth cannot digest. It never goes anywhere or breaks down to become something else in the circle of life (*Lion King* wheeeee!). It's being found everywhere on Earth, including places untouched by man, like the freezing polar ice caps (penguin and polar bear land) and the darkest depths of the ocean (miiiiiiiles deep). Whole worlds that exist, that we can't see or hear, are being affected by us. It's kind of like farting in your bedroom and someone in Africa calling you up to be like, "Dude, we have never met, but that STINKS."

WE USE
5 TRILLION
PLASTIC BAGS...
PER YEAR!
THAT'S 160,000 A SECOND!
AND OVER 700 A YEAR
FOR EVERY SINGLE PERSON
ON THE PLANET.

As plastic floats around the oceans, it chokes the marine life, killing 1 million seabirds and 100,000 marine mammals and turtles EVERY YEAR. In fact, scientists think that in a hundred years' time we could lose up to half of all the species on the planet if we do not slow down our destruction. The animals that we are used to seeing and the fish in the oceans may not be there in the future, because they do not have time to adapt to the environment that WE are changing. We may have to get used to eating jellyfish fingers because those dudes will THRIVE with no turtles to eat them!

SO, IN SUMMARY . . .

⚠ KILLS FISH, BIRDS, AND ANIMALS

⚠ DAMAGES OXYGEN-PRODUCING PHYTOPLANKTON

⚠ GETS INTO THE FOOD CHAIN

SO THAT'S ALL PRETTY GROSS AND HORRIFYING, BUT SOON WE'LL BE ON TO MY FAVORITE PART OF THE BOOK — HOW WE CAN MAKE A CHANGE!

A PLASTIC BAG IS USED FOR AN AVERAGE OF 12 MINUTES (WHEN YOU RUN TO THE STORE).

TIP: A bag for life will last for YEARS before you have to throw it away. Hooray!

BUT AFTER YOU
CHUCK IT AWAY
IT CAN TAKE
UP TO
20 YEARS
TO DECOMPOSE.

THE ATTENBOROUGH EFFECT

David Attenborough. Legend. National treasure. All-around great guy. You've probably heard of him. He's my hero. He is going to crop up a lot through this book, with many of the people we've interviewed naming him as their science hero. And for good reason — the dude is amazing, and his natural history documentaries have changed everything about the way we look and think about our planet. Here's some more information about everyone's favorite broadcaster:

SIR DAVID ATTENBOROUGH WAS BORN IN WEST LONDON ON MAY 8, 1926. THE SAME YEAR AS QUEEN ELIZABETH II!

HE IS THE ONLY PERSON TO HAVE WON BAFTAS FOR PROGRAMS IN BLACK-AND-WHITE, COLOR, HD, AND 3-D.

THERE'S ONLY ONE TYPE OF ANIMAL HE DOESN'T LIKE . . . RATS!

IN 1985 HE RECEIVED A KNIGHTHOOD FOR HIS WORK, GRANTING HIM THE TITLE SIR DAVID ATTENBOROUGH.

AT LEAST 15 SPECIES OF PLANTS AND ANIMALS HAVE BEEN NAMED AFTER HIM.

Attenborough has written and presented nine series of documentaries about the Earth's animal and plant life. The series *Blue Planet* and *Blue Planet II* both focused on the ocean, and *Blue Planet II* gained the highest UK viewing figures for 2017: 14.1 million. Wow! No wonder so many people are waking up to the problem of plastic in our oceans. By showing us the evidence of what plastic is doing to our wildlife (such as the albatross chick ingesting a plastic bag in *Blue Planet II*), he has made the effects of pollution impossible to ignore.

Sir David's not done yet—in March 2019, he presented an "urgent" film documentary about climate change for BBC One called *Climate Change — The Facts*. The one-off film focused on the potential threats to our planet and the possible solutions. Attenborough says "conditions have changed far faster" than he ever imagined when he first started talking about the environment twenty years ago.

MEET
DR. LUCY WOODALL

TELL US WHO YOU ARE AND WHAT YOUR JOB IS

Dr. Lucy Woodall. I am a marine biologist at the University of Oxford and principal scientist of Nekton.

WHAT DO YOU DO?

I am interested in the patterns of life in the marine world and how humans interact with it. I run scientific expeditions to identify the most important aspects to help with achieving sustainable management and conservation. I spend about four weeks a year at sea. The rest of the time I am working in the laboratory and office, teaching students and interpreting data for marine governance bodies nationally and internationally.

HOW DID YOU GET INVOLVED IN IT? WHAT WAS YOUR PATH TO THIS JOB?

I was always interested in identifying the rock-pool creatures during my summer holidays in Devon, England, as a child. Inspiring teachers and lectures, and later a drive to be part of the solutions for a sustainable ocean, led me to want to understand the ocean-life systems and share this with those in power.

WHAT HAS BEEN THE PIVOTAL MOMENT IN YOUR CAREER?

While looking for small roundworms in deep-sea sediment I saw tiny fibers in an array of colors. I had an "Aha!" moment—"What if they are plastic?" I thought. This was in 2012, before the majority of media interest in marine plastic. From this simple observation we have continued to tackle some of the unknowns associated with plastics as part of the research conducted in my laboratory.

WHAT ARE THE BEST AND WORST THINGS ABOUT PLASTIC?

Best = versatility. Worst = it is not costed across all its life cycle (we need to learn to value it properly).

WHO IS YOUR SCIENCE HERO?

Because I did my PhD in the field of conservation genetics, this has to be Rosalind Franklin. Born in 1920, Rosalind Franklin was a British scientist who helped discover DNA!

WHAT IS YOUR FAVORITE ANIMAL?

I need pages for this . . . Well, I am currently in Antarctica, so I should choose something that lives down here. As I have been fortunate to see the seabed below the waves and ice, I will choose a feather star (crinoid). It is related to the sea star, but has very delicate arms that look a little like feathers (they hold their arms off the seabed to catch their food). It is their swimming that is totally mesmerizing. Check them out!

MEET
WILL TRAVERS OBE

TELL US WHO ARE YOU AND WHAT YOU DO

I'm Will Travers, president of the Born Free Foundation, which is a wildlife charity. I'm a campaigner because I see things in the world that I'm unhappy with and I try to change them. I know that I can't do this on my own, so I find people who think like me and we all get together and change it.

HOW DID YOU GET INVOLVED IN WHAT YOU DO?

It was a bit of an unusual path—in the 1960s my mom and dad were the actors in the film *Born Free*, so we went to Kenya when I was five. I guess I got used to the idea of wildlife and Africa and everything. When in 1983 an elephant was put to sleep at the London Zoo (the last African elephant there), we set up a little charity to investigate what had happened . . . That was thirty-five years ago!

WHAT HAS BEEN THE PIVOTAL MOMENT IN YOUR CAREER?

It took Born Free twenty years of campaigning to get the European Union to agree that all zoos have to be licensed. There are 3,500 zoos in Europe and every zoo now has to meet certain standards—for animals, the public, conservation, and for education. It's not good enough, but it's a start!

WHAT ALTERNATIVES TO PLASTIC DO YOU USE? WHAT'S YOUR BEST SWAP?

Find as many alternatives as you can and, if you are buying something with no alternative, think how you might be able to repurpose the plastic. I'm vegan and eat a lot of avocados, and they tend to come in a little plastic shell. I hold on to the shells and I'm intending to use them as seed planters for my garden in the summer.

Born Free has been building nighttime stockades for livestock (cows, sheep, and goats) in parts of Kenya to protect them from lions and hyenas. We use recycled plastic made into poles, which is far more durable than wood, which gets eaten by termites. The plastic poles will last forever. What's not to love about plastic, sometimes.

WHAT'S YOUR TOP TIP FOR MAKING A DIFFERENCE?

The first thing is to understand that we can ALL do something, even in a tiny way. I'm keen on creating space for wildlife — it could be a window box that you've chosen flowers for because they're great for pollinators, such as bees and butterflies. Or if you've got a garden you could do the same. Or you could join a community center and restore a small area that would be good for insects or birds. We can all do something, however small. The biggest mistake you can make is thinking you can't do anything.

Also think about what we buy, where we spend our money, the organizations we support, the people we champion . . . Sir David Attenborough, Chris Packham, Michaela Strachan, Bella Lack — support these people.

WHAT IS YOUR FAVORITE ANIMAL?

I've worked a lot around elephants — I spent nearly thirty years campaigning against the ivory trade, have had a baby elephant in the back of my car, rescued elephants from being killed, nearly been killed by an elephant at least twice, but that doesn't make me love them any less. Elephants are extraordinary — and, if you look after them, all the other species that share their habitat are looked after, too.

"IF WE CAN REDUCE THE AMOUNT OF RUBBISH IN OUR RIVERS BY 20 PERCENT EACH YEAR, IN SEVEN YEARS, WE WOULD GET THE ENVIRONMENT IN BETTER BALANCE."

—MARCUS ERIKSEN, FOUNDER, 5 GYRES

THIS IS THE COOLEST PART . . . YOU ONLY NEED TO CHANGE A FEW ITSY BITSY TINY THINGS TO MAKE

A HUGE IMPACT

ON OUR PLANET'S WELLBEING.

And I really mean that. Just a bit of knowledge and action is all it takes. I don't think anyone is expecting the entire nation to turn into a beach cleanup crew overnight (although that would be rad). You can start small and work your way up. That's what I did. Literally.

First I went through all my toothpastes, face scrubs, and any other toiletries that I thought might contain microplastics. Lo and behold, I found a whole bunch listed in the ingredients of the brand of toothpaste I had been using. This grossed me out. I had been brushing my teeth with tiny pieces of plastic for as long as I could remember.

I switched to a toothpaste that didn't contain any of those ingredients. Phew. Luckily none of the face scrubs and soaps I'd been using contained plastic, but they were in plastic containers. So I simply switched to bars of soap, body wash, face scrub, and shampoo (yeah, they do all come in a bar!).

In the kitchen I changed all my plastic wrap to beeswax wrappers or reusable silicone covers.

For out and about I got myself a few water bottles and reusable coffee cups. They now do these rad coffee cups that squish down so you can put them in your pocket!

For shopping I take a reusable bag or I just shop at places that provide paper bags.

I guess the only major thing I have noticed about the way that I shop now is that I prepare before I even leave the house. That's it. No big deal really.

Then I started to (politely) inform my friends, family, and now, well, pretty much everyone about how they could change their habits. Honestly, it never takes much. When I see a friend using a plastic cup all I have to say is, "Do you know that plastic cup is going to outlive you?" That usually gets people thinking.

The coolest thing about taking action that I have found is, apart from the companies profiting from single-use plastic, I am yet to meet a fellow human who wants to continue being part of the problem.

GOOD STUFF!

THIS IS WHERE YOU GET TO DECIDE HOW FAR YOU WANT TO TAKE IT.

You can do something as small as cutting plastic bottles out of your daily routine. So your action could be not to use the plastic and buy a reusable bottle to carry with you. If you are out and about, choose drinks in cans or glass bottles. You can take it further and let others know about the plastic bottle they are about to drink from and encourage them to recycle, not throw it away.

Or write to drinks companies letting them know you would like them to stop using SINGLE-USE plastic bottles. This direct approach worked when a leading brand of chips launched an awesome recycling scheme after consumers mailed them back their empty chip packets, complaining that the packaging was non-recyclable.

Remember the microbead petition I told you about at the beginning of this book? If enough people rally together, the people at the top will HAVE to listen. After all, we are their customers, right? It would be like me playing a song that nobody liked onstage and everybody BOOing. I would sure enough stop playing that one and play another! (This happens whenever I go near a microphone.)

Sometimes cutting down your plastic footprint may take a little bit of planning and thinking ahead. Like, "Will I be needing water today . . . ? Yes . . . or I will pass out," or, "I'm going to prepare my lunch at home and take it in a reusable lunch box," or if you're going shopping: "Maybe I should take a reusable bag with me so I don't need a plastic one at the other end." Sometimes it's making small changes at home that make a huge difference to the environment.

There is a whole bunch of alternatives to single-use plastic. You just have to look a little harder than normal sometimes. The great thing is that in the long run you will probably end up saving money as well as the planet! You can even get bamboo computer keyboards now!

A HUGE PERCENTAGE OF OUR PLASTIC WASTE COMES FROM OUR HOMES. OVER THE NEXT FEW PAGES ARE THINGS YOU CAN DO THAT WILL MAKE A MASSIVE DIFFERENCE.

BATHROOM

HOW MUCH PLASTIC IS THERE IN YOUR BATHROOM?

Have a look at the table on the next spread and see the swaps you could make. Remember to check the packaging of scrubs and toothpaste for microplastics. You need to look out for:

POLYSTYRENE,

POLYETHYLENE,

OR

POLYPROPYLENE

in the list of ingredients—they're the bad guys!

THINK ABOUT THINGS LIKE:

HOW MANY PRODUCTS IN PLASTIC BOTTLES ARE CURRENTLY IN YOUR BATHROOM?

HOW MANY BOTTLES OF SHAMPOO DO YOU USE EVERY YEAR?

HOW MANY THINGS IN PLASTIC DOES YOUR FAMILY USE TO GET READY EVERY MORNING? LOOK AT YOUR DEODORANT, TOOTHBRUSH, SHOWER GEL, BODY LOTION, HAIR PRODUCTS . . . IT'S PROBABLY MORE THAN YOU THINK!

 **TIP:** You probably do have lots of products made of plastic or with plastic packaging. Don't worry; finish these up first and then make sure you recycle them. Once that is done, see how many swaps you can make.

It's not always easy to get hold of the replacements (although stores are getting better at stocking this stuff, hooray) so don't worry if you can't make all the changes at once. Even if you do just one of these things it will already be making a difference. Especially if you encourage your whole family to make the same switch.

 TIP: There are some amazing plastic—free bloggers and vloggers you can follow for extra tips—check out the interview with Kate Arnell on page 88.

BATHROOM SWAPS

Plastic hair brush and comb → Wooden hair brush and comb

Liquid shampoo and conditioner → Buy large bottles that last longer, find a shop offering refills if possible, or use a shampoo bar

Liquid soap and shower gel → Use bar soap with paper wrapping

Toothpaste → Switch to microplastic-free or use tooth powder

Plastic toothbrush → Bamboo toothbrush

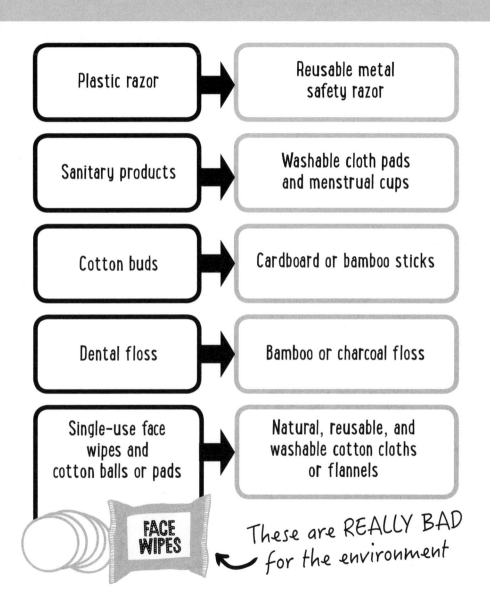

Plastic razor	→	Reusable metal safety razor
Sanitary products	→	Washable cloth pads and menstrual cups
Cotton buds	→	Cardboard or bamboo sticks
Dental floss	→	Bamboo or charcoal floss
Single-use face wipes and cotton balls or pads	→	Natural, reusable, and washable cotton cloths or flannels

FACE WIPES

These are REALLY BAD for the environment

THE AVERAGE PERSON BUYS A NEW TOOTHBRUSH EVERY 3 MONTHS.

SO THAT'S 4 WE'RE EACH THROWING AWAY EVERY YEAR.

ADD THE OTHER MEMBERS OF YOUR FAMILY AND SUDDENLY THE NUMBER SHOOTS UP!

TIP: Swap your toothbrush for an eco-friendly bamboo one!

KITCHEN

NOW LET'S TAKE A LOOK IN THE KITCHEN.

There is likely to be loads of plastic around here, too, in your utility cupboard and in the fridge! A good rule of thumb with food is to buy in bulk, to take your own bags and containers to local stores, or seek out food items in jars or cardboard. You can buy dish soap, hand soap, and fabric softener in five-liter bottles and keep refilling them.

NON-FOOD KITCHEN SWAPS

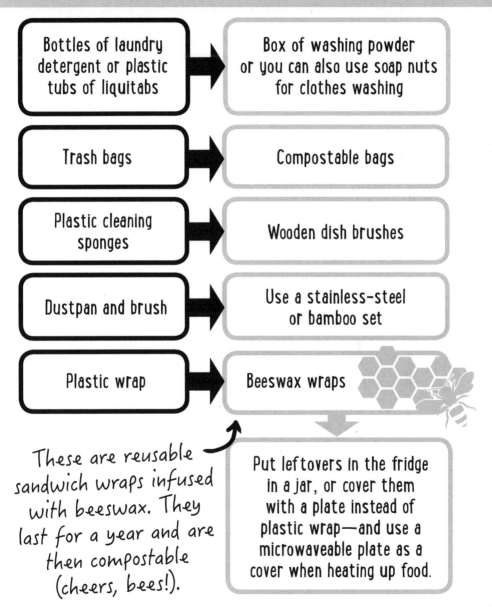

Bottles of laundry detergent or plastic tubs of liquitabs	→	Box of washing powder or you can also use soap nuts for clothes washing
Trash bags	→	Compostable bags
Plastic cleaning sponges	→	Wooden dish brushes
Dustpan and brush	→	Use a stainless-steel or bamboo set
Plastic wrap	→	Beeswax wraps

These are reusable sandwich wraps infused with beeswax. They last for a year and are then compostable (cheers, bees!).

Put leftovers in the fridge in a jar, or cover them with a plate instead of plastic wrap—and use a microwaveable plate as a cover when heating up food.

FOOD AND DRINK

KITCHEN SWAPS

Milk in plastic bottles	Milk in glass bottles— see if there's a milkman in your area who can deliver.

Who knew they contain plastic!

Like it's the '80s!

Tea bags	Use loose-leaf tea and a teapot. You can also get a reusable metal tea ball.
Plastic coffee pods or to-go coffee	Use ground coffee (bought in bulk) and a French press
Plastic-wrapped fruit and veggies	Buy fruit and veggies loose
Butter in plastic cartons	Buy a butter dish so that you can purchase butter wrapped in greaseproof paper
Cheese wrapped in plastic	Cheese wrapped in paper

AT THE SUPERMARKET

♻ Use reusable metal tins to purchase meat and deli items without packaging.

♻ Use reusable cloth bags for loose produce—baked goods and bread, for example, and for buying food loose in bulk, such as pasta, grains, snacks, etc.

♻ Look for fruit and veggies contained in their own peel, e.g. bananas, avocados. Or you can get a weekly delivery of a fruit and veggies box. Some supermarkets sell wonky veggies in boxes.

♻ Look for things in jars and boxes.

♻ Buy the biggest bags of dried items, such as pasta and rice, as you can and decant into smaller containers at home.

♻ Instead of individual yogurts, buy a big pot and decant into jars at home.

♻ Use paper mushroom bags to transport loose fruit from supermarkets and grocers instead of plastic.

ZERO WASTE

HOW TO MAKE A DELICIOUS, PLASTIC-FREE PACKED LUNCH!

Cloth napkin ....

Banana—comes with its own packaging! ....

Sandwich wrapped in beeswax paper
or a reusable sandwich wrap ....

Cookies, taken from the big packet at
home and stored in a reusable container ....

Yogurt, stored in a glass jar.
Eat with spoon from home! ....

Refreshing drink of your choice in
reusable bottle. No straw required! ....

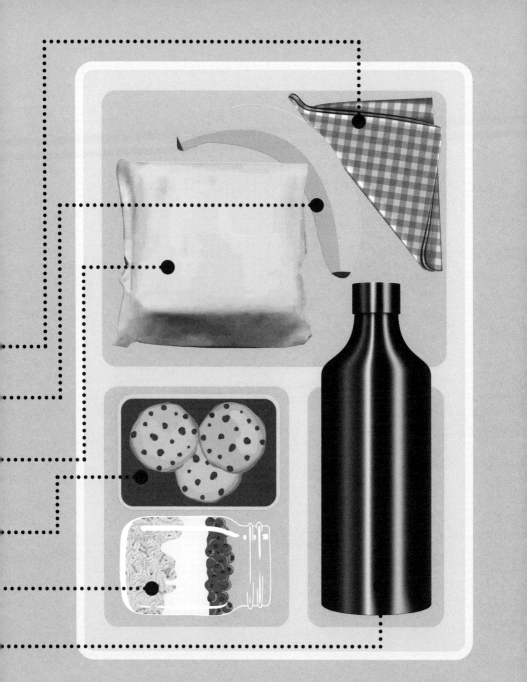

PARTIES AND

As well as the bathroom and kitchen items, there are dozens of other things around the house that contain plastic, so make sure you keep an eye out for those crafty little items you might not think about!

Here's an example from home — my mom is one of the loveliest, kindest, sweetest people I know, but even she gets it wrong sometimes. She's obsessed with the little plastic "Happy Birthday" things you stick in cards then laugh about as they fall all over the place when the person opens the card. These things stick around. Believe me, I know. I'm still finding "Happy 16th"s around my house! Of course, since then I have educated Mom about the problem and I can tell she is planning a more eco-friendly form of attack on my next birthday.

It's not just my mom (let's not put all the blame on her) — so many party items are single-use plastics. **BALLOONS**, **PARTY POPPERS**, and **CONFETTI**. It's quite a weird thing to think that things we use to celebrate life could actually be taking life once we are done with them.

Lots of **WRAPPING PAPER** contains plastic — especially the shiny, glittery kind. Watch out for glittery greetings cards, too, and choose a recycled paper design instead.

FESTIVITIES

STICKY TAPE is plastic, too. Where possible use string or ribbon to wrap your parcels.

And while we're feeling festive . . . **TINSEL AND ORNAMENTS** are usually full of plastic, so why not hang Christmas cookies or strings of popcorn from the tree?

TIP: BUY YOUR MUSIC DIGITALLY. As a musician it kills me to say it but it's better for the environment for all our music and film to be downloaded and not in physical form :-(

TIP: DITCH THE PLASTIC PENS. Invest in a refillable pen.

PLASTIC-FREE

Bring food from home in reusable containers—birthday cake included!

To avoid using plastic cutlery (which is often thrown away at the end of the day), you could serve loads of yummy finger food, like mini sausages on wooden sticks and tiny pizzas.

Have a giant bowl of chips poured from one big bag, rather than lots of individual bags.

PARTIES

Skip the balloons, or don't have too many!

If you are giving your guests party bags, use paper bags instead of plastic ones. A paper bag filled with sweets (bought in bulk) would make a great gift.

Avoid glittery wrapping paper and plastic confetti. Why not make your own gift wrap—get some brown paper and doodle all over it!

TIP: Have fun! It's hard to go completely plastic-free at parties, so don't worry if you can't follow all these tips. Even cutting down on one balloon will make a difference!

BRING YOUR

When I'm out for the day, I try to pack the following few items to ensure I have a plastic-free day. Why not build your own kit?

○ **A COLLAPSIBLE CUP WITH A LID** that I can use to get a hot drink. They fold down and don't take up too much room in your bag.

○ **A STEEL BOTTLE TO FILL WITH TAP WATER.** Metal carriers also stop chemicals from plastic leaching into water.

○ **A REUSABLE CONTAINER** of nuts or a banana if I want a snack.

○ **A SPOON OR SPORK** so that if I do end up buying food when I'm out, I don't have to use any plastic cutlery.

○ **A METAL STRAW**, which you can wash at home and reuse.

○ **A FOLDABLE REUSABLE BAG.** What did our grandparents and great-grandparents do before plastic was invented? They took bags made of other materials from home. I can remember my great-nan pushing a cart full of food home from the supermarket well after the explosion of plastic. Nice one, NAN!

OWN KIT

DON'T WORRY if you don't manage to do this every day. Every little thing you can do is a HUGE help to the planet.

If you are out and about without your kit, try to use a paper straw, ditch the lid and stirrer if you get a hot drink and buy a drink in a can or glass bottle.

WHERE POSSIBLE, TRY TO AVOID:

 STRAWS

🙁 PLASTIC CUTLERY

🙁 PLASTIC FOOD WRAPPING

MEET
KATE ARNELL

I'm Kate Arnell (née Edmondson) and I have a blog and YouTube channel — Eco Boost — sharing swaps and changes I've made to cut plastic and live a more zero-waste lifestyle. I worked as a TV presenter for ten years, but was thinking of different careers when I read a newspaper article about a family in California who could fit their annual garbage into a one-liter jar. I was already passionate about choosing organic, but felt increasingly frustrated with the amount of single-use plastic packaging my husband and I were throwing away as a result. I picked up a copy of *Zero Waste Home*, written by Bea Johnson, the mother of the family featured in the article, and set about making changes to how I shopped for food and the beauty products I used and refusing things we didn't really need as much as possible.

I decided to channel my new passion for zero waste into a YouTube channel, as I found that not many people were talking about it in the UK at the time. I was keen to make it fun, non-preachy, and more about "here's what worked for me" instead of "here's what you should do!" People often tend to take things too seriously when it comes to lifestyle changes, but I wanted to show you don't have to be perfect to make positive swaps and changes. I started about four years ago and have now become one of the main people in the UK talking about how to reduce waste through simple everyday choices and actions.

I also give talks and write a regular magazine column talking about ways to reduce waste.

HOW DID YOU GET INVOLVED IN IT? WHAT WAS YOUR PATH TO THIS JOB?

I started out as a TV presenter—my first gig was at MTV and then I went on to host various things from CBBC, the National Lottery, and BBC America's YouTube channel. I then set up my own channel on YouTube, talking about how to reduce waste and trying alternatives to plastic. My path has very much been driven by my passions.

WHAT HAS BEEN THE PIVOTAL MOMENT IN YOUR CAREER?

I think finally doing something that aligns with my values. I loved meeting Bea Johnson when I hosted a talk she was doing a couple of years ago, as it was her book that really transformed the way I see the world and how I operate in it. I also love getting positive feedback from people via Instagram and YouTube, who have said I inspired them to start making waste-saving changes in their lives.

WHAT ALTERNATIVES TO PLASTIC DO YOU USE?

I use a lot of reusables instead of disposables and generally look for items that come packaged in glass or metal, which can be more easily reused or recycled than plastic, or a product packaged in compostable cardboard that can be easily composted at home.

SINGLE BEST SWAP?

The menstrual cup—even friends who aren't remotely interested in reducing waste have tried it and now swear by it.

SINGLE BEST ACTION YOU CAN TAKE?

Embracing positive habit changes—remembering to refuse plastic freebies (straws, samples, gifts, etc.) and remembering reusables as much as possible. Also, customer feedback! It has such a big impact. Just don't be ranty about it. A polite email, tweet, or letter will do nicely.

WHAT IS YOUR TOP TIP FOR MAKING A DIFFERENCE? CAN YOU GIVE US AN OBVIOUS EXAMPLE AND SOMETHING A BIT MORE OFF THE WALL?

Lead by example! People follow actions more than instructions. Live your values and do things for yourself, and others will feel inspired. Don't preach or guilt others into doing things.

Return to sender! Send unwanted plastic packaging back to the company with a note as to why you are doing so.

WHAT ARE THE BEST AND WORST THINGS ABOUT PLASTIC?

BEST: It has been really useful in the medical world; it's light and durable. We just need to stop using it in such a disposable way.

WORST: We associate it with convenience and disposability because of how cheap it is and we don't have good-enough systems in place to cope with the sheer amount of it. It's linked to polluting our environment and our health and, in many cases, its use is not necessary. It has crept into everything.

WHO IS YOUR SCIENCE HERO?

Dr. Mark Hyman—I like that he uses his platforms (e.g. his YouTube channel) to discuss our relationship with food mostly, but also touches on how food, environment, and health are all connected. I like that he is pro-meat and he interviews really interesting experts with a lot of talk around sustainability and health.

WHAT IS YOUR FAVORITE THING ABOUT THE EARTH?

How the whole ecosystem works effortlessly together. Everything depends on something else to thrive and, without our modern systems interrupting those cycles, it functions beautifully. I also love the sheer beauty and diversity of the landscapes, from deep canyons to deserts, mountains, forests, and countryside.

WHAT IS YOUR FAVORITE ANIMAL?

I'm most fond of rabbits, I think, thanks to the pet house rabbit we had growing up. Although, alpacas, pigs, and dogs all rate quite highly, too.

BEACH CLEANUP

Many of our planet's beautiful beaches are in need of a serious cleanup, and plastic debris is a huge part of the problem. There are different sources for this pollution: items of plastic can be left on the beach, flushed down sewers, thrown overboard from boats, or washed down into the sea via rivers and other waterways. So the actual pollution often happens inland as well as near the water. But once the plastic enters the ocean it can then be washed back up on to our beaches.

As a result, both land and sea creatures are affected. Beaches are home to animals (like birds, sea lions, and sea turtles) who depend on clean land to survive. Marine animals are also affected by trash on beaches because when the tides rise the plastic items on the beach are collected up and taken back out to sea, where the marine animals might eat or be injured by the plastic.

This is where you can do something.

The next time you're on a beach or coastline, look out for the plastic items that should NOT be there, and pick them up (it's best to wear gloves) and take them to a recycling bin. That's the beginning of a BEACH CLEANUP! Use the power of social media to spread the word and post pictures about the garbage you have found on our precious beaches. Or start a beach cleanup with your friends or class at school—you would be surprised at how awesome you feel afterward. Whenever I am lucky enough to be near the ocean, I always pick up what I can carry.

THERE IS SOMETHING ABOUT KNOWING YOU HAVE NOT ONLY MADE THE BEACH LOOK A LOT COOLER BUT THAT YOU MAY HAVE SAVED AN ANIMAL'S LIFE, TOO, THAT'S VERY REWARDING.

WHY IS PLASTIC BAD FOR
MARINE ANIMALS?

Plastic doesn't disappear when it enters the ocean. Over time, it breaks down into tiny pieces called microplastics (remember them from the introduction?). Microplastics look and smell like food to many creatures, including sea turtles, seagulls, dolphins, and whales. These guys don't know how to tell the difference between a yummy jellyfish and a floating plastic bag. And eating all this plastic can be deadly. Plastic can fill them up so much that they can no longer eat actual food, causing starvation.

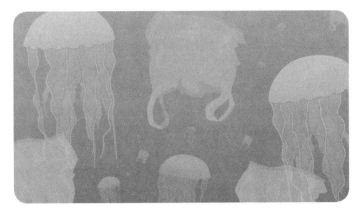

Plastic also looks like a home to sea creatures. During a recent expedition to the Great Pacific Garbage Patch (a concentrated area of plastic trash in the middle of the Pacific Ocean), the crew found evidence of fish, crabs, and barnacles living in nets, plastic water bottles, and body-care product packaging. Not cool.

According to a recent study, plastic pollution affects at least 700 marine species, while some estimates suggest that at least 100 million marine mammals are killed each year from plastic pollution.

HERE ARE SOME OF THE MARINE SPECIES MOST DEEPLY IMPACTED BY PLASTIC POLLUTION—THESE ARE THE GUYS THAT NEED OUR HELP THE MOST.

1. Sea Turtles

2. Sea Lions and Seals

3. Seabirds

4. Fish

5. Whales and Dolphins

THE MOST COMMONLY FOUND ITEMS IN BEACH CLEANUPS

Plastic bottle caps

Drinks cans

Metal bottle caps

Food wrappers

Plastic bottles

Plastic grocery bags

Glass bottles

Straws and stirrers

Other plastic/foam packaging

Cigarette butts

BEACH CLEANUP SAFETY TIPS:

 Do not go alone.

 Make sure someone knows where you are going and what time you plan to be back.

 Be aware of the tide and don't allow yourself to get cut off.

 Wear protective gloves or use a litter picker. If you can't, wash your hands afterward.

 Do not pick up anything organic that is not beach litter, e.g. dead animals, birds, or poo.

 Dress appropriately for the weather and wear good footwear (no open shoes or sandals).

 Dispose of your finds properly. Some plastics may be recycled. Please check locally what can and can't be recycled.

SPREADING THE WORD

One of the best ways you can help tackle the plastic problem is to talk to two or three people about it. Then encourage them to pass the message on and on!

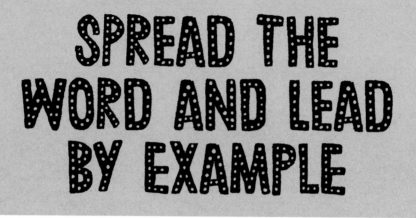

SPREAD THE WORD AND LEAD BY EXAMPLE

TELL YOUR FRIENDS. People your own age are probably more likely to listen to you rather than a boring grown-up (like myself).

TELL FAMILY. Some of your family are probably not as aware and as forward-thinking as you. I'm sure they will be shocked at the amount of plastic they have thrown out over the years.

WRITE LETTERS AND EMAILS. You would be surprised by the effect this can have. Companies do not want to be named and shamed, so why don't you let them know that you're unhappy!

WHENEVER POSSIBLE, REFUSE PLASTIC. You know when plastic, like a straw, is offered, you can say "ARE YOU CRAZY?" . . . or just politely say "no thanks."

START A PETITION or seek out petitions that are already running and sign those. That's exactly how the microbead got banned: Lots of people signing a petition saying they no longer wanted plastic in their TOOTHPASTE!

Dear [name of company],

I was shopping in my local branch of your supermarket last week, and was disappointed to see the amount of plastic used to wrap the fruit and vegetables. Please would you consider using less, for the sake of our planet?

Here is a photo to show what I mean. I would like to keep shopping with you but this excessive use of single-use plastic might make me shop elsewhere in future—and tell my friends to do the same.

Thank you for your time.

[your name]

ONE, MAYBE?

HOW MANY

IS THAT

IN A YEAR?

1 X 365 DAYS =

SO FOR YOUR WHOLE CLASS

(MADE UP OF, SAY, 30 STUDENTS)

THAT'S A WHOPPING

10,950

BOTTLES A YEAR!

At least 80 percent of these plastic bottles will end up in landfill or the ocean.

TIP: Get yourself a reusable bottle and make a HUGE difference.

MEET
DARA McANULTY

TELL US WHO YOU ARE AND WHAT YOUR JOB IS

My name is Dara—everyone calls me Naturalist Dara. A naturalist is someone who is curious to learn about nature. It's the most natural thing in the world—we can all be budding naturalists! I live in Northern Ireland. Well, I'm fourteen so I don't have a job or get paid, but I try to save the world—it's my passion and when I'm older I'll keep on doing it!

WHAT DO YOU DO?

I write a nature blog called Naturalist Dara: It's a diary about all my experiences, all the work I do—such as beach cleanups, litter pickups, and campaign work. I'm an ambassador for the Jane Goodall Institute, the RSPCA, and the #iwill campaign. I attend a lot of events, telling grown-ups off for the state of our planet—okay, not really, I politely tell them our world is in awful shape and ask them what they are going to do about it. I run an eco group at school called Roots and Shoots, and at every possible moment I try to tell people how magical nature is and how beautiful our planet is—so please stop trashing it! Hmmm, actually, when I write it all down, I wonder how I fit in time for school—but I do, because looking after and caring for our world is one of the most important jobs there is!

HOW DID YOU GET INVOLVED IN IT? WHAT WAS YOUR PATH TO THIS JOB?

I have always been curious about nature. It is fascinating. I knew that early on and I didn't stop thinking it. Then I read and learned so much and the thing is, once you are fascinated, then you learn and then ... you care, you fight for what you love, and you become so passionate it becomes your fire. I think young people's voices are really important—we haven't really known failure yet, so we take risks and we speak the truth. We can also see the world with fresh eyes, so it's important for adults to listen to us and remember that the child in all of us is a beautiful thing—honesty, compassion, and curiosity can actually save the world, I think. I started writing and many people liked what I wrote. I raised my voice, my anger, my frustration, my joy, my hope, my wonder. My blog won a few awards and now I'm writing a book called *Diary of a Young Naturalist*. Now lots of people ask me to talk about how to help young people do what I do. I want *everyone* to do what I do!

WHAT HAS BEEN THE PIVOTAL MOMENT IN YOUR CAREER?

Can I have a career at fourteen?! Yes, I can, because you're never too young to make a difference! The pivotal moment was actually when I saw a dead whale on the news, with more plastic in its stomach than anything else—this told me that there were things going on in the world that are killing wildlife without us realizing. As well as all the other work I was doing, I got obsessed about picking up garbage. I helped make our school canteen plastic-free and I started asking cafés to use paper straws and compostable packaging. It became an obsession. This wasn't enough, though. Educating people—that is where the power lies. Inspiring others to make a difference by changing a few habits—that's crucial!

WHAT ALTERNATIVES TO PLASTIC DO YOU USE? SINGLE BEST SWAP? BEST ACTION THAT YOU CAN TAKE?

Okay—so we never buy water bottles, ever. No plastic shopping bags and no single-use cups for Mom and Dad. We also have paper bags for fruit and veggies and we try our very best to cut down on all the other plastic packaging—*but* supermarkets do not make it easy for us! Single best swap—reusable water bottle! But the best action you can take is becoming more aware and educating yourself. Once you do this, change will follow. You won't be able to sit back if you truly know the damage your choices are making.

WHAT IS YOUR TOP TIP FOR MAKING A DIFFERENCE? CAN YOU GIVE US AN OBVIOUS EXAMPLE AND SOMETHING A BIT MORE OFF THE WALL?

Speaking your mind! Don't be afraid to tell grown-ups off—politely, of course. Write letters to your representatives and other people in power, such as supermarkets. Once, we collected over one hundred plastic gloves on our beach cleanup and we made it into a message—"Wake Up"—and sent a picture of myself and my siblings standing behind it, thumbs down, to every representative here in Northern Ireland and the UK. We sent it by email, and we got quite a few responses.

WHAT ARE THE BEST AND WORST THINGS ABOUT PLASTIC?

The plastic used in medicine makes sure people have clean and safe treatment. This saves lives. Also, technology—this helps keep people connected and makes the world more open and welcoming; if used properly, of course!

The worst—the overconsumption of plastic water bottles. For most of us, it's just unnecessary!

WHO IS YOUR SCIENCE HERO?

Alan Turing—he combined all the sciences to make knowledge accessible. He made a machine called the "bombe," which broke code more effectively during World War II, he invented the first computer (the Automatic Computing Engine), and he did so much research into mathematical biology and the foundations of DNA research. Scientists who combine many areas of science make connections that can save our world. If Turing was alive today, he would be coming up with amazing solutions. I just know it!

WHAT IS YOUR FAVORITE THING ABOUT THE EARTH?

Everything! I love the way everything is connected: humans, animals, trees, air, sea, space . . . It's all interconnected! We can't live without five out of six of those things!

WHAT IS YOUR FAVORITE ANIMAL?

Oh gosh! That is hard. I have to say that it's our native bumblebees—they are pollinators and so make sure our crops grow. Without bees, we have no reliable food source!

MEET EMILY PENN

TELL US WHO YOU ARE AND WHAT YOUR JOB IS

My name is Emily Penn, and I'm an ocean advocate and skipper.

WHAT DO YOU DO?

I have dedicated my career to tackling ocean plastic. I give talks all over the world on plastic pollution, I work with companies on reducing their plastic use, and I run eXXpedition—a company that organizes all-women sailing trips focused on examining plastics and toxins in the ocean.

HOW DID YOU GET INVOLVED IN IT? WHAT WAS YOUR PATH TO THIS JOB?

My journey began ten years ago, when I hitch-hiked around the world on a bio-fueled boat to get to a new job in Australia. It was a job I didn't end up taking. Instead, shocked by finding plastic in some of the most remote places on our planet, I chose to live on a group of Pacific islands for six months to organize a community cleanup.

I then traveled to California to learn more from some of the experts in the field of ocean plastic. In 2014, I launched eXXpedition and we have run eleven voyages so far. In autumn 2019, we will launch eXXpedition Round the World. This two-year project will take three hundred women sailing over thirty voyages to look at ocean plastic and its impacts.

WHAT HAS BEEN THE PIVOTAL MOMENT IN YOUR CAREER?

Appearing in an Apple advertisement. It opened up a lot of opportunities to talk about the plastic problem on a bigger stage.

WHAT IS YOUR TOP TIP FOR MAKING A DIFFERENCE?

Sit down, work out what your skills are (I like to call it your superpower), and how you can apply it to make a difference. This might be organizing a community or school cleanup, but it could be designing a poster for your school or college, putting together a short video highlighting the challenges of plastic pollution, sharing your actions on social media, or looking at how you might be able to use your love of science to make a difference in the future.

WHAT IS YOUR FAVORITE THING ABOUT THE EARTH?

That nature is so resilient, particularly our ocean. The Earth knows exactly how to fix itself, we just have to give it the space to heal.

WHAT IS YOUR FAVORITE ANIMAL?

Octopus — did you know they have nine brains? One in each tentacle and one in their head!

"NEVER FEEL YOU CAN'T MAKE A DIFFERENCE.
SOMETIMES THE ISSUES ARE PRESENTED IN A VERY SCARY WAY THAT CAN MAKE YOU FEEL HELPLESS— BUT WE AREN'T."

—ANDY BOOL, SEA LIFE TRUST

4

THE CULPRIT LINEUP

Recycling is a good thing, obviously, but not as much plastic as you might think is recycled.

Today, 95 percent of plastic packaging, worth a whopping $117 million a year, gets used once and is then thrown away. Of that, 14 percent is collected, but most of it is lost in the sorting and processing phase.
Another 14 percent is burned to produce energy.

Almost three-quarters of all plastic packaging is not recovered at all: 40 percent is landfilled, and 32 percent ends up as pollution.

RECYCLING SYMBOLS:
WHAT DO THEY ACTUALLY MEAN?

These symbols are pretty universal. We have all seen them at the bottom of our bottles or somewhere on the label. I had seen these little dudes on things for years, but I honestly had zero idea what they all meant.

So I did some research and it turns out they do mean something (it's quite important) and you don't need to have studied hieroglyphics to understand them. Different plastics are made from different things. Some are more harmful than others to the environment and break down slower, and some can only be recycled with their own kind (because of the chemical makeup and density) so it's important we take a little time to understand.

NAME: PETE OR PET (POLYETHYLENE TEREPHTHALATE)

Used for: food and drink packaging, e.g. water bottles, peanut butter jars, and single-use to-go food containers.

PET can be turned into literally anything, such as brand-new containers or even carpet! (So if you recycle that bottle of lemonade you have at lunch it could end up back in your house as carpet!) This plastic is considered the most valuable, but sadly it's not often recycled—so let's make sure that changes.

NAME: HIGH-DENSITY POLYETHYLENE OR HDPE FOR SHORT

Used for: ice-cream containers, juice bottles, detergent bottles, plastic shopping bags and shampoo bottles.

When this bad boy is recycled it can become things like drain pipes, benches, or a fence. It is an amazing material when used responsibly, as it's hard to break down and lasts for ages—but those qualities make it harmful to the environment, too.

NAME: VINYL (YUP, THE THING THE OLD FOLKS USED TO LISTEN TO MUSIC ON THAT'S NOW SUPER POPULAR AGAIN. EVEN WITH PEOPLE WHO DO NOT OWN RECORD PLAYERS.)

Used for: music, clear food packaging, cosmetics bottles, and medical equipment.

Vinyl is not recycled that often and for a GOOD REASON. Vinyl contains phthalates, a chemical used mainly to soften the plastic, but unfortunately it's harmful to people. This type of plastic should never be burned or used to cook with. You know what? Maybe we should just stay away from this one altogether!

NAME: LOW-DENSITY POLYETHYLENE

Used for: black trash bags, squeezable bottles, and plastic wrap.

Unfortunately this type of plastic can't be recycled, so AVOID IT IF YOU CAN!

NAME: POLYETHYLENE, OR PP TO ITS FRIENDS

Used for: medicine bottles, chip bags, microwave-meal containers, and tubs for dips.

PP can be recycled back into trays, bins, rakes, bicycle racks, landscape borders, ice scrapers, brooms, battery cables, and signal lights. PP plastic is often used to carry hot food and liquid as it has a higher melting point than other plastics.

NAME: POLYSTYRENE

Used for: you will find this dude carrying your eggs, CDs (if you're retro), and keeping your packages safe in the mail.

This stuff is considered the worst of all to recycle so it's a villain! But the award for the SUCKIEST of all has to go to:

NAME: PLASTIC THAT CONTAINS THE CHEMICAL POLYCARBONATE. THIS CHEMICAL HAS BEEN LINKED TO HORMONE DISRUPTION AND REPRODUCTIVE PROBLEMS IN LIVING THINGS (IF EATEN).

Used for: big water-cooler bottles, iPods, and laptops.

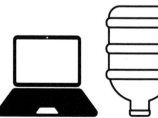

At least many of its uses are not SINGLE-USE, but this is also in nylon and some food containers, which can be dangerous!

It's important that we try to sort the good from the bad (and the ugly), because we come across these different plastics every day. I try to look at this sorting a bit like my music playlists: They all come under the MUSIC category, but I try to separate Susan Boyle from my heavy metal, like Bring Me the Horizon.

Though recycling doesn't necessarily get rid of our problem, it does soften the blow and change how we think about plastic. It's easy to see how this small action can have a huge impact and why some of the things you were throwing into the recycling bin are still ending up in landfills or the ocean.

BUT FIRST, you need to check what you can recycle where you live . . .

YOUR FRIENDLY NEIGHBOURHOOD PLASTICS

The good news is that 99 percent of UK local authorities now offer to collect your recycling along with the regular trash. You can check online at the recycling locator — **Earth911.com** — what type of plastic your area recycles. Make sure you only put the things they do take into your recycling bin and look online to find out how to safely dispose of the rest.

Once you have correctly recycled your plastic and waved it off with the garbage dudes or at the recycling bank, your work is done. The baton is then handed over to the recycling facility where the plastic is sorted by polymer type and then eaten up in a giant plastic-eating machine. The machine then spits out the now-shredded plastic and it is washed and melted and turned into pellets about the size of a lentil or grain of rice. These cool little pellets can be sold on to environmentally conscious companies who use LOCAL PLASTICS. Companies like LUSH only use these and never make their own plastic. The pellets can pretty much be turned into anything, which is really incredible if you think about it.

More and more hard-to-recycle products now have their own collection schemes — Boots has started collecting contact lenses and packets, Walkers has a chip bag recycling scheme, and there's a really cool company called TerraCycle, which (as well as running the Boots and Walkers schemes) recycles everything from toothpaste tubes to old pens. Go to **terracycle.com** to find out how you can get involved.

RECYCLING AROUND THE WORLD

The plastic bottle recycling rate was about 45 percent in the **UK** in March 2018, less than the 90+ percent in **Germany** and **Sweden**. This is due to a very successful bottle-and-can deposit return scheme in those countries. By using a "reverse vending machine," consumers can return their bottles and cans and earn a small sum. Once returned, the retailers are responsible for properly recycling the containers. The great news is this scheme is now being introduced in the **UK**—so look out for reverse vending machines cropping up in supermarkets near you and get ready to earn a bit of cash!

As well as the reverse vending machines, **Germany** has a pretty awesome system in place called the Green Dot system. Green Dot works by having the manufacturers and shops pay a penalty for the packaging. So the more plastic on a product, the higher the penalty. This means the people making the plastic are contributing to the funding of the recycling. The Green Dot system has led to less plastic and paper, and thinner glass and less metal being used to make packaging, which means less trash is left over after you have used the product.

Wales has the fourth-best recycling rate in the world. It has set itself ambitious recycling targets, aiming to achieve zero waste by 2050.

A 2017 study showed that **Europe** recycles 30 percent of its plastics, compared to just 9 percent in the **United States**, but the majority of plastic waste still winds up in landfills and in the oceans.

Many countries have started to ban plastic bags (one step up from charging for them, like in the **UK**). In **Morocco**, the second-largest consumer of plastic bags after the **United States**, nearly 500 tons of plastic bags were seized or confiscated after their ban came into effect in 2016.

Plastic cutlery has been banned in **France** and the **Seychelles**. No need to recycle something that doesn't exist in the first place!

People in **Austria** are really good at sorting waste: 96 percent of them separate their packaging waste from general waste. Austrian households sort and collect more than one million tons of packaging and paper waste each year. Their government makes it easy for people to recycle cleverly—consumers are provided with several different bins and there is a recycling pickup service for 1.6 million households.

In **Switzerland**, you have to pay a tax to use the landfill. Most importantly, there are special gray bags to hold waste that you have to pay for. **Switzerland** now has one of the best recycling results in the world.

Sweden is recycling its waste so efficiently that they are now importing waste from other countries. They are using a system where they turn waste into usable energy. A quarter of a million homes in **Sweden** are using electricity and heat that is produced from this recyclable waste.

DAVID KATZ
AND THE
PLASTIC BANK

David Katz is the cofounder of the Plastic Bank, which was set up in 2013 in Vancouver, Canada, with the aim of stopping plastic waste from entering the world's oceans. Cleaning the oceans is the very last thing we should be doing, Katz says. Instead, we should be stopping them from being polluted in the first place.

"If you were to walk into a kitchen and the sink is overflowing, water spilling all over the floor, soaking into the walls . . . you're going to panic; you've got a bucket, a mop, or a plunger," he says. "What do you do first? Why don't

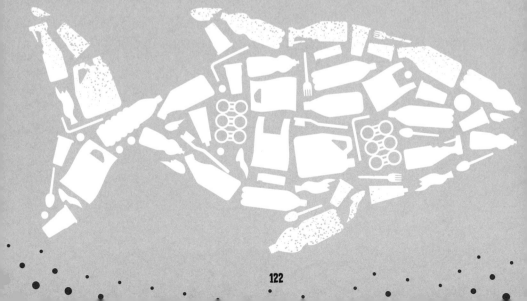

we turn off the tap? It would be pointless to mop or plunge or scoop up the water if we don't turn off the tap first. Why aren't we doing the same for the ocean?"

The Plastic Bank works in many of the world's poorest countries, such as Haiti, Indonesia, and the Philippines—often places that don't have trash collections or processing systems like we do—and it pays people to collect waste plastic, giving them a way to earn money to feed their families. He calls the Plastic Bank "the world's largest chain of stores for the ultra poor."

The plastic they collect goes to sorting centers where it gets chopped up into tiny flakes and sent to Europe or America, where it can be made into new products.

The Plastic Bank also encourages some of the world's largest companies, including supermarket chains, to use ocean-bound plastic in their products. It does this by certifying that it is recycled plastic, which it calls "social plastic," that otherwise would have been dumped in the ocean. Some big companies have committed to go "plastic neutral," paying to build recycling plants in places where there aren't any now.

The Plastic Bank is trying to "close the loop" on plastic waste to make sure that it gets used again rather than ending up poisoning a whale or getting caught around the neck of a turtle. And it has plans to extend the scheme to allow people to hand in their plastics when they go to church every week. Given that there are 37 million churches around the world, that could make a huge difference.

The Plastic Bank is also working on schemes where shops can collect plastic and exchange it either for cash for the collector or, if you're handing it in in a rich country like ours, you can use it to help poor people on the other side of the world. "Now we can all be part of the solution and not the pollution," Katz says.

MEET LAUREN ST JOHN

TELL US WHO YOU ARE AND WHAT YOUR JOB IS

I'm a children's author and an ambassador for the Born Free Foundation. In March 2018 I founded Authors4Oceans, an alliance of more than fifty children's authors and illustrators who campaign against single-use plastic in the book industry, literary festivals, and schools. I was inspired to start Authors4Oceans shortly after watching *Blue Planet II*. I ordered a lemonade in a book store and it came with a straw in it. I thought that if I approached the management as an individual and appealed to them to stop stocking single-use plastic generally, probably not a lot would happen. However, it occurred to me that if me and some of my children's-author friends, all of whom are passionate about the environment, formed a group, together we could make a difference.

Authors4Oceans is now over sixty strong and includes some of the best-known children's authors and illustrators in the UK—Michael Morpurgo, Jacqueline Wilson, Chris Riddell, Katherine Rundell, Abi Elphinstone, Piers Torday, Dr. Ben Garrod, and Robin Stevens, to name a few. We campaign on a range of marine-conservation issues, from plastic packaging to overfishing and dolphins in captivity. Lots of publishers and book distributors shrink-wrap everything, and there are scores of booksellers and schools still dishing out plastic straws, bottles, and plastic bags. What we found immediately is that children, in particular, are absolutely passionate about stopping the plastic menace and saving our seas.

Little by little, we're persuading the book industry to look at their processes. Inspired by Authors4Oceans, one chain of bookshops radically changed their policy on single-use plastic in their cafés, replacing plastic straws with eco-friendly ones and phasing out plastic bottles. They sell reusable bamboo coffee cups, too.

It's so inspiring and gives me so much hope when I see the response to Authors4Oceans' initiatives, such as the "Oceans are NOT Rubbish" schools competition. Kids have had enough. They're telling us loud and clear that they don't want to grow up in an environmental wasteland. They want clean rivers and seas brimming with dolphins, whales, seals, otters, and healthy, happy birds. We need them to beg their parents to ditch single-use plastic and to be both their conscience and their memory. If they see a family member heading for the supermarket, we ask them to remind them to take tote bags, so they don't need plastic.

HOW DID YOU GET INVOLVED IN ENVIRONMENTAL ISSUES?

I grew up on a farm and game reserve in Zimbabwe and had a pet giraffe called Jenny. We were an animal-mad family and rescued lots of creatures, including a baby monkey and two warthogs — Miss Piggy and Bacon! At one point we had eight dogs, six cats, eight horses, the giraffe, warthogs, and a goat that we'd saved from a shelter. It was heaven!

Professionally, I was a sports writer for a long time for the *Sunday*

Times, then I wrote about music and used to travel around America interviewing country stars like the Dixie Chicks, Steve Earle, and Dolly Parton. Then I started writing children's books. My first, *The White Giraffe*, is about an English girl who goes to live on a game reserve, where she discovers she has a gift for healing animals. Writing it made me realize how much I missed helping wild animals. I approached Born Free and we started working together. I've rescued leopards and dolphins with them and returned them to the wild.

WHAT HAS BEEN THE PIVOTAL MOMENT IN YOUR CAREER?

Many of the best experiences of my life have involved nature and animals. For my book *Dolphin Song*, I went to the stunning Bazaruto Archipelago in Mozambique, and I once swam with a wild baby dolphin in Australia. I've also swum with sea lions and, by mistake, with great white and hammerhead sharks in the Galápagos Islands. Always read the brochure BEFORE getting in the water!

I feel very fortunate. I left school at sixteen with no qualifications, but after studying journalism a whole world opened up to me. I was a sport and music journalist for years, but also did investigations. I'm most proud of an exposé I did for the *Sunday Times* on the so-called dolphin "entertainment" industry.

WHAT ALTERNATIVES TO PLASTIC DO YOU USE? SINGLE BEST SWAP? SINGLE BEST ACTION THAT YOU CAN TAKE?

It's the tiny things that make the difference. If you're sitting in your living room in London, say, you're not going to imagine that the ring pull off your milk or orange-juice carton is going to end up in the Pacific. But what if it did? Or what if it found its way into your local river or a bird's nest? Take a second to snip through ring pulls or plastic can holders, so that even if they do get into nature they won't end up choking birds or fish. Plastic toothbrushes are a menace too. Consider bamboo or metal.

WHAT ARE THE BEST AND WORST THINGS ABOUT PLASTIC?

Good: One famous brewery makes plastic beer crates that last up to ten years. Then they return to the factory, where they're melted down. Two hours later, they're a new beer crate. That's plastic functioning well and not harming anyone.

Bad: Balloons are an environmental nightmare. They're fun for humans, but not animals. They choke and kill scores of fish and birds.

WHO IS YOUR SCIENCE HERO?

David Attenborough. He's an amazing human who has inspired millions of people to care about our planet and want to save it.

WHAT IS YOUR FAVORITE THING ABOUT THE EARTH?

The diversity of it, and the extraordinary lives of animals. Two years ago I went to Hwange National Park in Zimbabwe. From a wildlife hide, I watched four elephants lean together in a bonding hug. I was at their feet and I could feel the love between them. I'll never forget it.

WHAT IS YOUR FAVORITE ANIMAL?

Horses, dolphins, elephants, rhinos, and small cats, lions, and tigers. I'm fascinated by smart animals and birds. The emotional intelligence of elephants and dolphins is breathtaking.

HOW LONG UNTIL IT'S

CARTON
3 months

PLASTIC SHOPPING BAG
20 years

APPLE CORE
2 months

FOAM BUOY
50 years

NEWS

NEWSPAPER
6 weeks

WOOL SOCKS
1–5 years

FISHING LINE
600 years

PLASTIC BOTTLE
450 years

MEET BLUE OLLIS

TELL US WHO YOU ARE AND WHAT YOUR JOB IS

My name is Blue and I run the Blue Ollis YouTube channel, social media platforms, blog and website, ebooks, newsletter . . . and soon to be even more!

WHAT DO YOU DO?

I promote personal and societal holistic wellbeing through vegan activism, sustainability, plant-based eating, and self-care.

WHAT IS YOUR TOP TIP FOR MAKING A DIFFERENCE? CAN YOU GIVE US AN OBVIOUS EXAMPLE AND SOMETHING A BIT MORE OFF THE WALL?

The best way to make a difference is by starting with yourself. That is, looking at your own waste and getting creative with ways you can reduce it every day, little by little, then by making changes that impact others, like picking up litter when you see it, even if it's not yours. Carrying an extra tote bag to the store and giving it to someone who is reaching for a plastic one and telling them about reusables.

WHAT ARE THE BEST AND WORST THINGS ABOUT PLASTIC?

The best thing is that we don't need it. The worst thing is that it'll be here forever, killing animals (us included) and polluting our homes for eternity.

WHAT IS YOUR FAVORITE THING ABOUT THE EARTH?

That She naturally provides us with everything we need!

MEET
JONATHON PORRITT

TELL US WHO YOU ARE AND WHAT YOUR JOB IS

I'm Jonathon Porritt, the founder-director of a sustainability organization called Forum for the Future. We work globally with large organizations to help them find solutions to creating a sustainable future. Telling people, "Yes, you *can* make a difference."

HOW DID YOU GET INTO THIS?

I was a teacher for ten years and have been a member of the Green Party since 1974. Even though I was teaching English I was always bringing environmental issues into the classroom!

WHAT HAS BEEN THE PIVOTAL MOMENT IN YOUR CAREER?

Attending the 1992 Earth Summit in Rio de Janeiro — I spent two-and-a-half weeks there and met tons of people from sectors like business and farming, people I'd seen as the "enemy" and suddenly they were all saying yes, we really do need to do something about these challenges. It was brilliant. I came back and set up two organizations to work with that positive energy.

WHAT'S YOUR TOP TIP FOR MAKING A DIFFERENCE?

For young people: Be aware of your influence. If you apply a little bit of effort and imagination, it's amazing how quickly you can make a change.

The first port of call for companies is to use innovative ways to transform their packaging. We have seen more innovation in the last two years than in the preceding twenty years.

The government has to help too: We could and should be recycling far more plastic than we are at the moment. Our government needs to force local authorities to do a better job.

WHAT ARE THE BEST AND WORST THINGS ABOUT PLASTIC?

There are some fantastically good uses for plastic, which we would be unwise to forget. Plastic is not evil. Durability is one of its great benefits. Its cheapness is enormously important, for instance in improving food safety and food hygiene. But we have to manage plastic use more intelligently. We've been so slow to address this.

We need to look at both the design *and* disposal ends of the process. You have to design every single item so that it can be easily broken down and repurposed. Design for better plastic use is really exciting from a creative point of view.

WHO IS YOUR SCIENCE HERO?

James Lovelock—the guy who came up with the Gaia hyphothesis. His work led him to the conclusion that the Earth was one integrated system. Everything influences everything else, so if you change one bit of that system there are subsequent effects in another part of the system. He got pilloried by scientists for his beliefs at the time, but now everyone has bought into the theory. He was also a brilliant inventor and invented the machine that allowed people to measure tiny amounts of chemicals in the atmosphere. So when we started to get concerned about the ozone layer, his technology was crucially important.

WHAT IS YOUR FAVORITE THING ABOUT THE EARTH?

I'm a bit of a tree-hugger! I've always loved trees, and started climbing them at a very young age, much to the consternation of my parents! I spend as much time as I can walking in woods and forests. Back in the 1970s, I planted a seventy-acre tree farm in New Zealand—that was a lot of trees. I often encourage people to do a bit of wood-air breathing!

WHAT IS YOUR FAVORITE ANIMAL?

Slime molds—tiny little organisms that live on the forest floor. When the food's run out, they come together to form a pillar, that explodes out to colonize new areas!

WERE YOU GOOD AT SCIENCE AT SCHOOL?

No, hopeless! Physics I hated, chemistry—I learned equations until my brain hurt, but would immediately forget them after the exam. And I didn't do biology! Now as an environmental activist I work hard to keep up with science.

MEET
AMANDA KEETLEY

TELL US WHO YOU ARE AND WHAT YOUR JOB IS

Amanda Keetley, founder of Less Plastic.

WHAT DO YOU DO?

I raise awareness of the issues of plastic pollution in the ocean and what practical steps we can take to tackle the problem. My approach focuses on learning how to use less plastic in our daily lives —because the more plastic we use, the more will unfortunately end up in the environment.

135

I have developed a series of visual infographics to inspire people, schools, community groups, and businesses to use less plastic. I also offer talks and workshops, and I've written a book called *Plastic Game Changer.*

HOW DID YOU GET INVOLVED IN IT?

I moved to Devon, England, five years ago and was shocked to see for myself firsthand the scale of plastic pollution on UK beaches. I noticed everyday things I used in my life washing up on the beach and that was when I fully realized that we're all responsible in some way for the mess that is causing such devastation in our oceans.

I started Less Plastic as a part-time hobby, but it soon took over! I gave up my other work to focus on Less Plastic full-time and my aim is to create simple tools and systems to make it easier for individuals and businesses to make a difference.

WHAT HAS BEEN THE PIVOTAL MOMENT IN YOUR CAREER?

A pivotal moment for Less Plastic was when Greenpeace International picked up on my first infographic — "9 tips for living with less plastic" — soon after I first shared it on social media, mid-2016. They shared it again around Christmas to inspire New Year's resolutions. My social media following has grown steadily since that point and that was when I realized the full potential of my infographics for conveying complex messages in a really simple, visually appealing, easy-to-action way.

WHAT ARE THE BEST AND WORST THINGS ABOUT PLASTIC?

In some cases, plastic can be life-saving. My son has a peanut allergy and has to carry an EpiPen, which thankfully he hasn't had to use yet, but if he ever did need it I know we would be very grateful for that small plastic tube he has to take with him everywhere.

But it makes me really sad when plastic is used for single-use products or for meaningless junk like the clear plastic heart shapes some retailers were selling around Valentine's Day. I know it was just supposed to be a bit of fun, but it's so unnecessary in the scheme of life to manufacture large quantities of something that will give a moment's amusement before going in a landfill forever.

WHO IS YOUR SCIENCE HERO?

I really admire Professor Richard Thompson, head of marine litter research at Plymouth University. He was responsible for coining the phrase "microplastics" when he questioned where bigger plastic was ending up and discovered it was in fact breaking down into tiny pieces. The queen must admire him too as she awarded him an OBE last year!

WHAT IS YOUR FAVORITE ANIMAL?

I've always loved cats best, since I was old enough to know what animals were, but I now have a cat and a dog and it's really hard to choose a favorite!

"TALKING ABOUT **WHAT YOU CAN DO** IS A LOT MORE POSITIVE THAN SHOUTING ABOUT THE PROBLEM."

—ARIEL BOOKER, COFOUNDER, CANO WATER

5
SMELLS LIKE ENTREPRENEURIAL SPIRIT

entrepreneur

1   *a person who sets up a business or businesses, dares to make their ideas happen, and is usually very, very awesome.*

"Wow, did you hear about that kid's school project that's going to change the world? What an entrepreneur!"

So, now that we have a clear understanding of the state of our awesome planet, let's get down to what YOU can do to help save it.

You don't need to have a PhD, or be the smartest kid in class, or be the next Sir David Attenborough to have a huge, POSITIVE impact on our planet. All it's going to take is a tiny bit of willpower, a sprinkle of belief in yourself, and a giant tub-load of love for your home.

Let's take a look at what some regular people like me and you have done with their small ideas, and see how they turned them into realities.

BOYAN SLAT

When Dutch sixteen-year-old Boyan Slat came across more plastic than fish while scuba-diving in Greece, he decided to devote a high-school project to investigating ocean plastic pollution and why it was considered IMPOSSIBLE to clean up. This sparked Boyan's imagination and gave him the drive to come up with a solution.

His idea was simple. Use the ocean's gyres to bring the trash to us! Boyan invented a device — a U-shaped pipe (they call it "the floater" . . . haha!) — that drifts around in the middle of the ocean and catches all the trash floating on the surface. The invention requires no power, because all it needs is nature's own force to trap the debris. Once the device has rounded up all the plastic, ships go out and bring the garbage back to shore to be recycled.

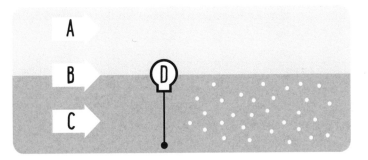

SIDE VIEW OF BOYAN SLAT'S "FLOATER" SYSTEM. SIMPLE BUT EFFECTIVE.

- A: Wind
- B: Waves
- C: Current
- D: Cross-section of floating barrier
- (Wind, waves, and current all act on the barrier, thus pushing it into the slower-moving debris, which is then moved only by the current.)

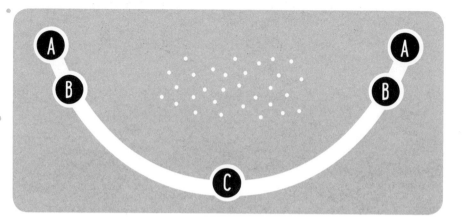

TOP VIEW OF BOYAN'S FLOATING BARRIER

- A: Navigation pod
- B: Satellite pod
- C: Camera pod
  (There are also nine lanterns situated every 100 meters along the barrier to provide visibility.)

Boyan founded the Ocean Cleanup in 2013 with just 300 euros of his savings—and by 2017 it had received over $31.5 million in donations! Things really took off when Boyan did a TedX talk about his vision, which was picked up by several news sites and then went viral. He ended his talk by saying, "We created this mess . . . so please don't tell me we can't clean it up together." The first $90k was raised in a matter of days via crowdfunding.

Boyan is now the CEO of the Ocean Cleanup, and his device is predicted to clean up HALF of the Great Pacific Garbage Patch by 2025.

How awesome is that? A kid's idea went from being a small school project to the largest ocean cleanup in history!

TWO DUDES

While I was attending a fashion event (by attending I mean standing there awkwardly) in London a few years back, I was approached by two young dudes waving cans at me. I almost bolted in the other direction. I assumed they were handing out a new type of energy drink, until I heard one of them say: "It's CANNED water — an alternative to plastic bottles. We've been on our gap year, but have come back early to set up this idea. After the amount of plastic pollution we saw on our travels, we believe this is a much better, eco-friendly alternative to bottled water."

I was shocked. "You had me at CANNED," I replied.

The company, named CanO Water (see what they did there?), was founded by three friends — Ariel Booker, Perry Alexander Fielding, and Josh White, who were all under the age of twenty-five!

What these three friends have invented is so awesome. They haven't actually thought OUTSIDE the box — it's more like they've taken a look

at what's already INSIDE the box. Rather than scratching their heads, waiting for the "lightbulb" idea to come to them, they took the problem and came up with a solution in a very SIMPLE way. So when I started writing this book I knew I had to interview them to find out more . . .

WHO ARE YOU AND WHAT'S YOUR JOB?

We are Perry and Josh, two of the cofounders of CanO Water. Perry works on design and branding, while Josh handles the distribution, sales, and marketing. Ariel is the third cofounder and has a similar role to Josh: day-to-day logistics. We all come from different backgrounds and have different skills, which merge very nicely. We were friends first, though — we've known each other for over ten years.

HOW DID YOU DECIDE TO START A COMPANY?

A few different things came together . . . a design, awareness about the plastic pollution problem, going to Thailand and seeing plastic everywhere, even on islands that were empty: lots of plastic bottles, fishing nets, plastic lids, and other stuff the sea was spitting out. In London we don't see anything like this, so it was a shock and an eye-opener.

Perry wanted to make a can of water 'cause it was so cool from a design perspective. Nobody had done anything like that before. Our lightbulb moment was realizing that there was a purpose to the cool packaging.

TELL ME MORE ABOUT WHAT YOU DO

We educate people about why cans are better. Seventy percent of all aluminium mined in the 1800s is still in circulation. It's infinitely recyclable. After you've recycled it five or six times, plastic isn't clear any more — so it can't be a bottle. Cans can be recycled forever. People are always collecting cans because they'll get money from it with commodity schemes, and we've been brought up knowing that you recycle cans.

There are a lot of big people taking note of what we're doing and noticing that people are willing to spend a bit more money on something that's better for the environment. A lot of companies have now committed to stocking our cans instead of single-use water bottles, e.g. London Zoo.

We sell two types of canned water —with resealable and non-resealable lids. Drinking from the tap is the best alternative to plastic bottles, but something is needed for drinking on the go. Billions of people are used to buying something from the shelf and having a drink while they're out and about.

DID YOU HAVE ANY CHALLENGES TO OVERCOME?

When we first started, most people thought it was a fad. We had to get a distribution process and win the love of consumers. Through branding, events, social media, marketing —and *Blue Planet II* —we overcame lots of obstacles and learned a load of lessons. We could see there was more stuff about plastic in the newspapers, so we knew the demand was coming. But in the beginning people laughed at us. During the first year we had to make phone calls to owners of newsagents and explain we were selling water in a can —it was quite funny, and impossible to explain! And it was really hard; we'd left our jobs and we had no positive feedback at the start. Luckily, we launched with Selfridges after two months. There was this real moment of elation when we got in there, and in Whole Foods too.

DO YOU HAVE A SCIENCE HERO?

Neil deGrasse Tyson and David Attenborough—we've got a cardboard cutout of him!

NEIL DEGRASSE TYSON IS AN AMERICAN ASTROPHYSICIST, AUTHOR, AND SCIENCE COMMUNICATOR.

TELL US SOMETHING ABOUT CANO WATER THAT MIGHT SURPRISE US?

We are three [young] guys who've never done this before. We had no office for two years—we're not a huge company; we don't work in a skyscraper in New York. We really want to have fun with our brand, too.

WHAT'S IT LIKE WORKING WITH YOUR FRIENDS?

It's great. We disagree all the time, but the most important thing is to always keep moving forward because we're all working together for the same goal. We are all quite creative and we all like to pitch in with different things. It's healthy arguing!

Working with your friends makes it not feel like work. I'd be chilling with these people anyway! Teamwork makes the dream work!

MEET EDWIN BRONI-MENSAH

TELL US WHO YOU ARE AND WHAT YOUR JOB IS

I'm Edwin Broni-Mensah, the founder of a company called GiveMeTap. Our vision is that around every single corner of the world every human being will be able to access free drinking water, whether you're in the UK or in Africa. We do that by selling stainless-steel water bottles that allow you to access a network of cafes and restaurants that will give you free tap water, so you never have to buy a plastic bottle again. And every bottle that you buy gives a person in Africa five years' worth of clean drinking water, as we use twenty percent of our revenue to fund water projects there.

HOW DID IT START?

It all started with my own selfish ambition of wanting to get a six-pack. I wanted be in great shape before I turned twenty-five. So I was working out a lot and drinking around five liters of water a day. I was going to and from campus but stopping at cafés and restaurants to ask for tap water. This was back in 2009, and I was met with so much resistance from cafés saying, "No, buy a plastic water bottle. I don't want to give you my tap water unless you're a customer." And I couldn't really wrap my head around that. Added to that was the fact that my dad grew up in Ghana, where he didn't have easy access to clean drinking water. So I thought, *Okay, how can I help?* I wanted to find a way to help both people like myself and people who grew up like my father, without access to water. And that's how the company was born. It was like a project, initially, where I just wanted to map out all the restaurants that were kind enough to give you access to free water. And we would use part of the revenue we made to help others. I was doing that alongside my degree at the University of Manchester.

HOW CAN PEOPLE BUY YOUR BOTTLES?

You can buy them online. We have a few retailers, but most of our business at the moment is corporate. We are working with some of the biggest companies in the world to completely eliminate their use of plastic cups. These companies used to go through millions of cups every single year, but they wanted to cut down their plastic consumption so they decided to introduce GiveMeTap bottles, and they gave one to every employee.

HOW DOES YOUR APP WORK?

It is an online map showing the location of places that are happy to give you access to their tap water, without you being a paying customer. We want people to keep their reusable bottles with them, take it into any café or restaurant in the program and get free water, rather than buying a plastic bottle of water.

TELL ME ABOUT THE WORK YOU ARE DOING IN AFRICA

It started off in Namibia. My background is nothing to do with water — I'm a mathematician, I have a PhD in mathematics — and so when I started getting involved with funding projects I didn't have a clue what I was doing. I needed help! I met a woman called Marie Heyes, who used to run a company called Red Bush Tea, and her company had been building water wells in the southern regions of Africa for about fifteen years. She helped guide me and educate me on how to select partners and communicate with those communities we wanted to help, and so I went with her on one of her trips and we actually built a pump together in Namibia. And that was my first insight into what it took to really help these communities.

Then I did another project with Pump Aid in Malawi, to further understand the different types of pump infrastructure that could work in those regions. After those two pumps I decided to go back to Ghana, where my parents were from, to look at how I could help over there. In the last few years we've been doing projects with people in Ghana. We've got twenty-five projects coming up in the next few months, so we're having a massive impact now, which I'm so thankful for. It means access to water for yourself and others, and no waste in the world.

HAVE YOU NOTICED A CHANGE IN THE LAST FEW YEARS?

Absolutely. *Since Blue Planet II* came out (that was November 2017) it's been absolutely phenomenal. People are really trying to minimize their waste. And, of course, China is now saying that they're no longer accepting waste. And that's the same for many countries around the world. So what it shows is that when the governments add pressure and pledge to reduce the amount of waste they are generating in the first place, it can really make a difference. This trickles down to businesses, where we've seen the effect of introducing initiatives like the one that many coffee chains have, where they reduce the cost of the drink if you have your own cup—these things are really starting to make a difference.

WHAT DOES IT MEAN TO PEOPLE, TO HAVE FRESH WATER IN THEIR TOWNS AND NOT HAVING TO WALK MILES TO GET IT?

Water has an impact on everything and it changes everything within a community. When you don't have access to water, women and children end up walking miles and miles every day to go and get some. It means that you don't have time to go to school or get a job. Bringing water to a community changes all that. If you have a water pump at a school, it's actually going to increase attendance: More children want to go because they know that they can stay clean and hydrated.

Pumps are also used to irrigate the land so that the community can grow crops to eat and sell and start building up wealth themselves. You also reverse water-borne diseases, which is one of the biggest killers in all forms of life across the world. So you can instantly change that. Access to fresh water reverses all kinds of social issues.

And of course it has a positive effect on the plastic front. For example, in various regions across Ghana the water isn't clean enough to drink. So, to be able to drink water, it's common for people to buy plastic sachets of clean water from street vendors—one sachet contains maybe 200 milliliters of water, and they can cost a couple pennies to buy. The amount of waste that is generated from these sachets is unbelievable; they create mountains of plastic. And when you put clean drinking water in those communities you're reducing plastic consumption there as well as in England and America.

WHAT IS YOUR FAVORITE THING ABOUT THE EARTH?

Palm trees. And water. They have a special place in my heart. I was in Brazil a little while ago, on a small island, and I was surrounded by palm trees and water. It just gave me so much peace. And also human beings! I think we're all really cool.

Here's another cool person doing something really innovative: Adam Lowry, who cofounded Method Products in 2000.

You've probably got some of their eco-friendly cleaning products in your bathroom cupboard or kitchen cabinet.

Tired of sprays, liquids, and washes created from potentially harmful chemicals, Adam and his cofounder, Eric, decided that there must be a cleaner way to clean. Their products are all naturally derived, nontoxic, paraben-free, and biodegradable, and they even look good! The Method brand stands for green living, green energy, and sustainability, and they're also big fans of the anti-animal cruelty movement, so you can be sure that the products you clean with are helping to save the world in every way they can.

AWESOME!

MEET
ADAM LOWRY

TELL US WHO YOU ARE AND WHAT YOUR JOB IS

My name is Adam Lowry and I am the cofounder and CEO of Ripple Foods. Ripple uses unique technology to make plant-based foods delicious. Prior to Ripple, I cofounded and helped to run Method Products, which is now the largest green cleaning company in the world.

WHAT DO YOU DO?

At the highest level, I design and operate businesses where, the more they grow, the bigger the positive impact on people and the planet. A great example of this is the creation of the first 100 percent recycled plastic packaging, which we pioneered at Method over fifteen years ago. This eliminated 100 percent of the production of new plastic for our packaging, but also lowered the carbon footprint of our bottles by 75 percent, while at the same time making financial sense (since recycled bottles are far less carbon intensive, their prices don't rise in proportion to oil prices at nearly the same rate).

Method's Southside Soapbox is probably the world's most sustainable manufacturing facility. It's LEED Platinum certified (one of only two in the country), renewably powered, water neutral, and produces fresh leafy greens on its roof while it provides green manufacturing jobs in the city of Chicago.

HOW DID YOU GET INVOLVED IN IT? WHAT WAS YOUR PATH TO THIS JOB?

Combining business and impact really came out of my time as a climate scientist, working at the Carnegie Institute for Science in the mid to late '90s. My role there was to show what would happen to our Earth system as a result of climate change. Unfortunately, that work did not bring about meaningful action on climate change, and so I got pretty frustrated with that. I turned to business, the largest and most powerful institution on the planet, as the place where impact could be created. But it meant doing business differently. Method was born from that idea and I'm still very much following that passion of using business to create positive impact.

WHAT HAS BEEN THE PIVOTAL MOMENT IN YOUR CAREER?

That realization at Carnegie that, for me, I wanted to work on this problem in a different way.

WHAT ALTERNATIVES TO PLASTIC DO YOU USE?

Aside from the easy stuff like bags and bottles, I try to buy fresh and eat in rather than takeout. Fresh whole foods rarely need plastic packaging — think fruits and veggies — and they're better for you anyway.

WHAT IS YOUR TOP TIP FOR MAKING A DIFFERENCE?

I think the most important change we need to make is in our psychology around plastic. That's why at Method we created the first-ever packaging made out of plastic collected from the ocean. We did that really to tell a story about plastic and engage people in a discussion, and we did it through four short documentary films we produced and distributed. Recycled plastic by itself isn't a particularly interesting story, but, by showing you could create something beautiful out of something sad, we brought emotion and engagement to a topic that had previously been very dry.

WHAT ARE THE BEST AND WORST THINGS ABOUT PLASTIC?

Plastic is an incredibly important and valuable material. It's important not to make it the bad guy, because the alternatives often have consequences you didn't mean to happen (glass, for example, takes a lot more energy to transport . . .). We just need to be smart about where and how we use it. That means using alternatives where the lifespan of that plastic is very short (like single-use plastic), and then where we do use plastic, let's use the plastic we've already got — there are billions of tons of it on the planet already, so let's use that instead of making more — in other words, let's use recycled plastic everywhere.

WHO IS YOUR SCIENCE HERO?

I've become friends with Dr. Michael Braungart over the years. He's a brilliant chemist, but what he really does is challenge why things are the way they are. He understands and thinks about materials in terms of their past, their present, and what they will be in the future in a way that is unique.

WHAT IS YOUR FAVORITE THING ABOUT THE EARTH?

I'm always filled with a sense of wonder and amazement when I'm able to experience all that our planet can do, whether that's a vivid sunset, a beautiful coastline, or a thriving forest. It's alive and resilient, and stunning. I feel very connected when I get to experience those things.

WHAT IS YOUR REUSABLE BOTTLE MADE OF?

Stainless steel.

WHAT IS YOUR FAVORITE ANIMAL?

The octopus. I've been fortunate enough to see several in the wild. They are incredibly intelligent, adaptable, and infinitely fascinating.

These people have proven that taking action is far more doable than you would think.

Let's not forget that a great idea doesn't always just pop into your head by magic. It can sometimes take hundreds of other ideas to arrive at the AWESOME one. The most important thing is to remember that the journey to your own GREAT idea should be just as fun as arriving at the invention itself. So get out the drawing boards, pens, rulers, calculators, toilet paper, your imagination—anything you want—and get inventing!

SEA LIFE AND SEA LIFE TRUST

A: I'm Andy Bool and I'm the head of the SEA LIFE Trust. The SEA LIFE Trust is a global marine-focused charity, dedicated to protecting marine life and habitat across the world—we're partnered with Sea Life aquariums all over the globe and we run lots of animal sanctuaries as well. We have a seal sanctuary in Cornwall, where we see seals coming in affected by plastic. We had a seal pup recently who wasn't eating or feeding for a while, and actually this seal pup pooped out a plastic bag after a few days in the sanctuary—that was what was stopping her eating. She recovered fully after that, but it shows the extent of plastic pollution. We see a number

of seals coming into our sanctuary who are affected with similar problems.

Alongside that we're building the world's first open-water sanctuary for whales. It's in Iceland, and will provide a home for two beluga whales who are coming from an aquarium in China to live a more natural life in this bay.

J: My name is James Robson. I'm the senior curator at SEA LIFE London. If you don't understand what a curator is, probably the best way to describe it

158

is to say I'm like a storyteller; we tell a story with our collections. So if it's a natural history museum it's with bones and skeletons. Here at the aquarium, the animals tell that story.

HOW DID YOU GET INVOLVED IN IT?

A: When I was in my early twenties I went traveling to Australia and I started volunteering for an environmental conservation organization. It confirmed that I wanted to work for a charity and make a positive difference. And that was like twenty years ago! I'm now leading an environmental charity: the SEA LIFE Trust.

J: I'm one of those annoying people — I knew really young what I wanted to do. I saw a TV program featuring David Attenborough in a dinghy with a woman, and they were going out to look at sharks. He described her as a marine biologist. And as a kid I just went, "I want to be a marine biologist." And at secondary the teachers said, "Do science!" So I took all the sciences, and then I just became more and more specialized and ended up doing marine and freshwater biology at university, then went on and did a masters and now I'm doing a PhD.

WHAT ALTERNATIVES TO PLASTIC DO YOU USE? SINGLE BEST SWAP? SINGLE BEST ACTION THAT YOU CAN TAKE?

A: I used to use shower gel and shampoo and I took part in plastic-free July last year. That made me rediscover soap and I could see that reducing the plastic from shampoo bottles and shower gel bottles has made a big change in my life.

J: I have started buying products from LUSH. They have switched their messaging and made it much more local, saying things like, "Do lots of small changes. If you see litter, pick it up; make sure you put your litter away properly; try to reduce plastic use; switch from single-use plastic bottles to multi-use bottles, cans, soap." It makes people think, *Okay, what* *small things can I do day to day that will reduce the problem a little bit? And it's empowering just to be able to do that.*

WHO IS YOUR SCIENCE HERO?

A: Mine is Jacques Cousteau, the French scientist and ocean explorer. I grew up watching his programs, and absolutely loved them.

J: I had two. One was David Bellamy. He's a fascinating man, and so passionate about the environment. As a kid, I was obsessed! But the main one is Attenborough. And that's because he can make every topic interesting.

WHAT IS YOUR FAVORITE THING ABOUT THE EARTH?

A: The places where the mountains meet the sea. I love those places.

WHAT IS YOUR FAVORITE ANIMAL?

J: I'm obsessed with cephalopods—so that's octopus, squid, and one I really love is a nautilus.

A: I love seals, always have. They're just beautiful, stunning animals. And having the opportunity to rescue them, through the sanctuary, and seeing them released is just amazing.

WWF HQ— LYNDSEY DODDS

TELL US WHO YOU ARE AND WHAT YOUR JOB IS

I'm Lyndsey Dodds, and I'm the Head of Marine Policy at WWF in the UK. I'm a marine biologist, so that's what I studied at university and then I moved into working for WWF. I've got a team of experts that work on all issues to do with protecting the oceans, so that can range from looking at the way that fishing is carried out and making sure we've got enough protected areas in the oceans,

but also, particularly recently, there's been a lot of attention on the plastics issue and the impact it's having on the ocean.

HOW DID YOU GET INVOLVED IN IT? WHAT WAS YOUR PATH TO THIS JOB?

I've always had an interest in the ocean, and it sounds quite cheesy, but I can clearly remember at about eight years old, standing at the coast in Scotland and looking at the oceans and thinking, *Wow! What's in there? How do you find out what goes on?* So I had an interest in the oceans and then went to university and did a degree in marine biology there and then actually stayed at university, doing a PhD.

WHAT'S THE COOLEST THING YOU'VE HEARD OF FOUND AT THE BOTTOM OF THE OCEAN?

Every time there's an expedition something new is discovered so it really is that last frontier of science on the planet.

AMAZING. BUT WE'RE STILL FINDING PLASTIC IN THOSE DEEP PLACES?

That's the bad news, really—there's plastic even 4,000 meters down. They've found plastic in the deepest trenches of the ocean so it's really pervasive and prolific.

WHAT HAS BEEN THE PIVOTAL MOMENT IN YOUR CAREER?

Well, I had the pleasure of visiting an area—an island called South Georgia, which is very nearly in Antarctica. It's a subpolar island, so it really is in the middle of nowhere, which is kinda amazing. I saw loads of amazing wildlife, loads of penguins, fur seals, whales . . . so many incredible things! But, slightly depressingly, at the same time we could see that there, in the middle of nowhere, was still plastic on the beaches.

REALLY? AND WERE THERE ANY HUMANS ON THIS ISLAND?

Only the researchers who are based there. There are no populations. And there are also a lot of albatrosses, these giant seabirds that have their nests there. And we were hearing stories about these nests having pieces of plastic in them as well. Obviously albatrosses are foraging and picking up things from all over the place, bringing them back, feeding them to their chicks, and using them to line their nests.

SO THIS TRASH IS COMING FROM ALL OVER THE WORLD. WOW. SO IN THEORY A BIT OF PLASTIC YOU THROW AWAY IN ENGLAND COULD END UP ALL THE WAY DOWN THERE

It's definitely a global problem and of course the oceans are liquid so they move around and move everything with them. The way to address this really is to treat it as a global problem: It's not one particular country or sector or industry—it's a global problem we all need to tackle.

WHAT IS YOUR TOP TIP FOR MAKING A DIFFERENCE? CAN YOU GIVE US AN OBVIOUS EXAMPLE AND SOMETHING A BIT MORE OFF THE WALL?

I think it's about making the changes you can in your own life, but also perhaps spreading the word and looking for ways you can influence—each one of us has a voice that can influence our government. It might not feel like we do, but we do! We've got our local representatives and there are always ways to get attention and getting that voice way up to government to show that people want change—they don't want things to stay the way they are.

WHO IS YOUR SCIENCE HERO?

Well, with my oceans theme, there's a really amazing scientist called Sylvia Earl. She was the first woman to walk on the seabed in a pressurized suit.

WHAT IS YOUR FAVORITE THING ABOUT THE EARTH?

You might not be surprised, but it's probably the oceans! I really love the oceans and all the amazing wildlife that's there and I don't think people realize how important they are. I don't think people realize that every second breath we take comes from the oceans. It provides food, transport, energy, and of course covers three-quarters of our planet, so it's pretty important.

"HAVING THAT LITTLE SPARK OF INTEREST IS ENOUGH."

—DOUGIE POYNTER

6

BE LIKE THE BEES

Honeybees are pretty awesome creatures.

They communicate by doing a cute little dance, waggling their behinds, and spinning around in a figure eight (I do the same, but it's not as cute). This is how they tell the other bees where the best flowers are, but also where there's an awesome place to set up a new home. One bee will come across an area on a flight and return home to tell the others.

THE AVERAGE WORKER HONEY BEE ONLY MAKES ONE-TWELFTH OF A TEASPOON OF HONEY IN ITS LIFETIME (A TINY DROP).

A QUEEN BEE WILL PRODUCE AROUND 50,000 BEES THAT WILL SPEND THEIR LIVES COLLECTING NECTAR FROM FLOWERS TO BRING BACK TO THEIR HOME AND TURN INTO HONEY. IT TAKES ABOUT 556 WORKER BEES TO GATHER 1 POUND OF HONEY, FROM ABOUT 2 MILLION FLOWERS.

AN ENTIRE HIVE WILL PRODUCE AROUND 350 POUNDS OF HONEY IN FIVE YEARS.

Impressive, right? But why am I rambling on about bees, you ask?

Well, as we've seen, it takes thousands of bees and a whole lot of work to make a single jar of honey. And one bee's work seems very insignificant, but when you add all the work together, EVERY BEE COUNTS. I guess we could see the plastic problem a little like this.

You may see yourself as small and insignificant, as you are only one of 7.7 billion people living on this planet, but every piece of action you take is heroic. Every bit of litter you dispose of correctly, and every time you refuse to take that plastic bag or straw, could decide life or death for another animal. Every time you spread the word on plastic YOU ARE MAKING AN IMPACT. As I said at the beginning of this book, I am definitely no scientist or professor. I'm just a human who has an interest and a concern for the natural world and I'm trying to do a little "waggle" in the hope that you guys will do a "waggle" and the message will spread like crazy and we will all work together to make a

HUGE
DIFFERENCE.

ONE LAST Q AND A!

I hope you've enjoyed the interviews with all the cool people who are already making a difference. Now I've got one last interview to share with you . . . MINE! My publisher turned the tables on me and asked ME to answer the questions I'd been asking everyone else. EEK. Here's what we chatted about . . . Enjoy!

TELL US WHO YOU ARE AND WHAT YOUR JOB IS

My name is Dougie Lee Poynter. I'm the bass player of the band McFly.

WHAT DO YOU DO?

The majority of my life has been taken up with music. When you're in a band, life has a routine. We sit around, write songs, go into a studio and record those songs, then promote the record all over the world, then you tour it. You're doing the same thing in a different city every night. Then the cycle starts again, but you get so many opportunities to do lots of cool things too. Being in a band is one of the best jobs in the world.

I love touring because you get to see the world and you have a purpose for being there. We learn about different climates—like going to Japan and experiencing their winter. It's super dry and sunny, but freezing cold. Then the summers are really humid. We'd always get it wrong and wear shorts when it was freezing!

OF ALL THE PLACES YOU'VE VISITED, WHICH WERE YOUR TOP 3?

1. The Amazon. Touring South America, you take one short flight to Manaus, which is quite a young city, still developing, right in the middle of the Amazon. I had always wanted to go to the Amazon — we learned about it at school, the diverse life there, everything from big cats to poison dart frogs. We got to go on the Amazon river and swim with pink river dolphins. They're actually pink, and blind so they just bump into you. I won't lie, I was a bit scared! You see people swimming gracefully with dolphins on Instagram, but this was different, and there were also piranhas and leeches in the river! The dolphins were completely wild but had got used to humans and were interested in you.

2. Virunga volcanoes between the Democratic Republic of the Congo (DRC), Uganda, and Rwanda—these are national parks that are home to mountain gorillas and are perched on volcanic islands. These gorillas are different to lowland gorillas that we know a bit more about and are seen in zoos. But mountain gorillas have never done well in captivity so they only exist here. My most memorable moment was when I got charged at by a moody teenage gorilla! He looked me in the eye then screamed, I saw the spit come out of his mouth and his huge canines and the smell of BO. We had been told not to run in

this situation; you're supposed to get into a ball on the ground to show you're submitting! I felt a very primal fear and the experience gave me a profound respect for nature.

3. Great Barrier Reef. It was a magical place — we traveled out to sea for a couple of hours to get there. All of a sudden there are waves breaking in the distance, the sea level seems to drop and there's this reef in the middle of nowhere. You jump in with your scuba gear and it's absolutely booming with life and color, all over the ocean. Sharks, sea anemones, everything. The water is so clear and so warm. The patch I visited doesn't exist any more, which is tragic.

WHAT HAS BEEN THE PIVOTAL MOMENT IN YOUR CAREER?

In terms of my music career, it was realizing at around the age of twenty-two that having fun with every show we play is the most important thing. Don't be insecure. The more fun you have the more it translates to the

people who like the music—there's no front to it. McFly fans can tell we genuinely love each other, more than brothers.

As for conservation, being in McFly has allowed us do things with charities and meet all kinds of people. When WWF got in touch, I was so stoked that they wanted to work with me. I felt pretty helpless before, like there was always someone brainier to do the job better. But it turned out I knew more than I thought from traveling. WWF are the guys who got me to Uganda and Rwanda with the gorillas. When I went out there, there were 700 mountain gorillas and now there are 1,000. I don't know exactly what impact the documentary I made had, but it must have helped a bit by raising awareness.

I didn't hear much about ocean pollution growing up—so when I was introduced to 5 Gyres the plastic issue became my main thing. It's only within the past two years that this issue has snowballed—although scientists have known about this problem since the '70s. It will take something like *Blue Planet* with a voice like Sir David that the entire world trusts to make everyone aware.

AFTER THIS BOOK, ARE YOU GOING TO CONTINUE WITH THE JOURNEY OF SPREADING THE WORD?

Yeah—I have no idea where it will take me. I still have so many things I want to learn about, like birds! The amazing thing about nature is it never gets boring. There are so many species—plus I want to learn about all of Earth's history, tectonic plates, and outer space. That's all nature, too.

WHAT ALTERNATIVES TO PLASTIC DO YOU USE?

My reusable water bottle—number one. Even around the house, even though I have glasses at home, it's always with me. I also really like using beeswax wraps instead of plastic wrap. Made by bees—so cool.

WHAT'S THE SINGLE BEST ACTION YOU CAN TAKE IN THE BATTLE AGAINST PLASTIC?

Having that little spark of interest is enough—things might not happen right away, but if you have any interest in nature, inevitably you will do something for the right reasons and make a change. Any change will make a difference.

WHO IS YOUR SCIENCE HERO?

Sir David Attenborough! I'm like a Justin Bieber fan for that guy. He single-handedly invented the nature documentary. In real life he's everything you want him to be and more. He's a fountain of knowledge, the most genuine character I've ever met. If it weren't for him, I don't know if I would have shown an interest or had such respect for the Earth. The way he talks about nature is so captivating and inspiring—it draws you in. Even as a young kid my mom would put on *Wildlife on One*, and I would be praying that it was a reptile episode! We're lucky to have him.

WHAT IS YOUR FAVORITE THING ABOUT THE EARTH?

Interspecies dependency. A fancy way of saying we're literally all connected — an animal dying will feed the flora and fauna that we feast upon. It gives me a sense of security that I belong here, a sense of purpose. Animals just "are" and they're in the moment.

WHAT IS YOUR FAVORITE ANIMAL?

It depends on the week! I always go back to reptiles — including dinosaurs. Sauropods were like giant cows with long necks that walked on all fours. They were herbivores. I often look out of my window and feel blown away that these animals existed on our planet. I imagine them roaming in the garden. It's not some fairy tale, or a story like *Lord of the Rings* or *Star Wars*. It's like someone saying Darth Vader actually existed! That's how I feel about dinosaurs.

On the other end of the scale, I really love ants! They remind me a lot of people — I like looking down on a city, seeing them eating together and feeding each other — workers go out and fill up their stomachs and throw up into each other's mouths!

WHAT ARE YOUR HOPES FOR THIS BOOK AND THE IMPACT IT WILL MAKE?

I hope that it joins the growing movement to take care of our planet. This generation already feels really engaged with it. If it can inspire them, like Attenborough did for me, and that has an add-on effect, if it plants any kind of seed, then great. I just want people to know that essentially you *can* make a difference.

MEET THE EXPERTS

Adam Lowry, METHOD

Like all superheroes, Method founders Adam and Eric gained their powers after being exposed to toxic ingredients; toxic cleaning supplies, to be precise. Method was founded in 2001, after these two childhood friends decided to put their heads together and find a way to produce eco-friendly cleaning products. And they wanted these products to look good — really good — so that you wouldn't want to hide them under your kitchen sink. So they set out to save the world by creating an entire line of home cleaning products that wouldn't pollute the environment. Method is now part of the largest green cleaning company in the world. Rad.

methodhome.com

Amanda Keetley, Less Plastic

Less Plastic is a pretty cool website full of easy-to-action steps to help you use less plastic in your day-to-day life. Amanda lives in Devon, England, and she founded Less Plastic in 2015 because she hated seeing all the plastic garbage on the lovely Devonshire beaches. She decided to do something about it and make a difference, to reduce the amount of plastic waste her family produced and help others make that positive change as well. Check out the website for awesome tips on how you can help your school use less plastic.

lessplastic.co.uk
@AmandaKeetley

Anna Cummins and Marcus Eriksen, 5 Gyres

5 Gyres is a nonprofit organization with a twist — they investigate key unanswered questions about plastic pollution, using science to present the facts and create innovative solutions to the problems. Its founders, Anna and Marcus, met on a research expedition to the North Pacific Gyre in 2008, and soon after Marcus proposed to Anna, using a ring he'd made out of an old fishing line he had pulled from the ocean. Marcus then left on a three-month voyage — not on your average ship, but on a boat kept afloat by 15,000 recycled plastic water bottles! He wanted to raise awareness about plastic pollution, and this in turn led to the launch of the 5

Gyres Institute. Pretty cool, huh? 5 Gyres has done some really awesome things: Did you know that they were the first to discover that microbeads were polluting our waterways? They used this study to convince some massive companies (like Procter & Gamble, Johnson & Johnson, and L'Oreal) to stop using microbeads, which led to the law banning microbeads in the US!

5gyres.org

Blue Ollis, Blogger

Blue runs a brilliant blog about sustainable living through simple methods that suit every home and lifestyle — check out her website to pick up some top tips!

blueollis.com
@BlueOllis

Dara McAnulty, Environmental Blogger, Conservationist, and Activist

Dara is just awesome. He's fifteen years old and he is PROOF that kids really can make a difference and help save our planet. Dara started his blog, which focuses on the environment and wildlife, in 2016. He hoped that people, especially young people, would read his blog and get interested in and care more about nature. From there he's gone from strength to strength: His blog has won tons of awards, he's given loads of talks, has been a very proactive environmental activist, and he's now writing a book to get his message out further. Awesome stuff.

youngfermanaghnaturalist.wordpress.com
@NaturalistDara

Edwin Broni-Mensah, GiveMeTap

GiveMeTap was born when Edwin, the founder, decided he wanted a six-pack. To do this he needed to massively increase his water consumption, but he didn't want to buy a plastic bottle every time he needed a drink. Instead, he asked cafés and restaurants to fill up his water bottle using their tap water — but he was refused, again and again. So he decided to take matters into his own hands: He designed a reusable stainless-steel water bottle and mapped out all the water-friendly, free-refill cafés, shops, and restaurants in his area and added them to an app. Thus, GiveMeTap and the Water Network were created! The idea is that people can buy a bottle and use the app to find places that will give them a water refill for free! Awesome! GiveMeTap is unique because it not only reduces plastic pollution, but it also dedicates a portion of its revenue to building wells in African communities that previously had no access to clean drinking water. Go, Edwin!

givemetap.com

Emily Penn, Skipper and Oceans Advocate

Emily is dedicated to studying plastic pollution in the most remote parts of our planet, traveling far and wide across the globe to research the problem and create solutions. And she's done some pretty awesome things on her travels: She's led waste cleanup from a tiny Tongan island, looked for microplastics on a voyage through the Arctic, and has gone around the planet on a record-breaking bio-fueled boat (fueled by natural products, rather than fossil fuels!). She's an ambassador for Sky Ocean Rescue and runs an organization called eXXpedition, which organizes all-female sailing voyages to raise awareness of, and find solutions for, the environmental impact of single-use plastic. How does she fit it all in?!

emilypenn.co.uk

James Robson and Andy Bool, SEA LIFE and SEA LIFE Trust

SEA LIFE London is an aquarium that is partnered with the SEA LIFE Trust, a registered charity dedicated to the protection of marine wildlife and habitats. Together, they develop projects that support marine life all over the world. SEA LIFE is great because it has such a huge global presence, so through them the Trust can really get its message of conservation out, all over the world. They focus on running marine-life sanctuaries, marine protected areas, plastic pollution, and improved protection for seals, turtles, whales, and dolphins.

visitsealife.com/london/
sealifetrust.org

 Jonathon Porritt, Campaigner, Author and Sustainability Guru

Jonathon has been in the world of sustainability since 1974, so he's been doing amazing things in the fight to save our planet for forty-five years! He has been very involved in the Green Party, was the director of Friends of the Earth and is the cofounder of Forum for the Future. The idea for Forum for the Future came about after the Earth Summit in Rio de Janeiro in 1992, and it is now the UK's leading sustainable-development charity, working with businesses and governments around the world to create a sustainable future.

jonathonporritt.com

 Josh White, Ariel Booker and Perry Alexander Fielding, CanO Water

After a trip to Thailand showed them the brutal extent of plastic pollution, friends Josh, Ariel, and Perry founded CanO Water. Essentially, water in a can. Their aim was to launch a product that could combat the waste of plastic water bottles and bring bottled water into the twenty-first century by using something more sustainable than plastic. Not only are their cans resealable and awesome looking, but they are also made of recycled aluminium, which is in turn totally recyclable. So when you recycle your can it can end up back on the shelf within six weeks! Mind-bogglingly AWESOME.

canowater.com
@canowater

MEET THE EXPERTS

Kate Arnell, Blogger

Kate lives a zero waste lifestyle — pretty impressive, right? She uses her YouTube channel and blog, Eco Boost, to share tips about her way of life, along with her favorite eco discoveries. You should definitely check out her blog, where she shows you how to shop for food without the packaging, how to find great secondhand clothing, which makeup is nontoxic, and which amazing plastic alternatives will really make a difference. Kate's book, Six Weeks to Zero Waste, *is publishing in December 2019.*

eco-boost.co
@Kate_Arnell

Lauren St John, Authors4Oceans

Lauren is a children's author who grew up on a farm and game reserve in Zimbabwe, which inspired a deep love of the natural world and the bestselling White Giraffe *and* One Dollar Horse *series. As a child, she even had a pet giraffe! She is the founder of Authors4Oceans, an alliance of more than sixty authors and illustrators who campaign against single-use plastic in the book industry, literary festivals, and schools, and which aims to inspire children, teachers, and parents to love our seas and fight against plastic waste, overfishing, and dolphins and orcas in captivity. An ambassador for the Born Free Foundation, Lauren has helped rescue dolphins and leopards from captivity and return them to the wild. Lauren's latest novel is* Kat Wolfe Investigates.

authors4oceans.org

Lyndsey Dodds, WWF

Lyndsey is the head of Marine Policy at WWF, the world's leading independent conservation organization. WWF's mission is to create a world where people and wildlife can thrive together, by looking at why nature is in decline — the main issues they look at are our food systems and climate change. Through its work, WWF is creating a massive global movement where people really want to put nature first, in all the decisions we make in our day-to-day lives. WWF has over five million supporters from around the world and works in more than one hundred countries. WOW.

wwf.org.uk

Dr. Lucy Woodall, Marine Conservation Expert

Lucy is a marine biologist with a passion for the world under the sea. She is an expert in the life, threats, and sustainability of our oceans. She travels the world, trying to understand the impact that human beings have on marine ecosystems.

Will Travers OBE, Born Free

Will is the president of Born Free Foundation, which works to ensure that all wild animals — whether living in captivity or the wild — are treated with compassion and respect. In 1966, Virginia McKenna and Bill Travers (Will's parents) starred in the classic wildlife film Born Free, *and from there went on to make a number of wildlife films together. In 1969 they acted in* An Elephant Called Slowly *with an elephant calf called Pole Pole, who, after filming, was gifted to London Zoo by the Kenyan government. In 1982, rumors circulated that Pole Pole, just a teenager, was going to be euthanized. Virginia and Bill did everything they could to stop this and launched a campaign to give Pole Pole a better life, but, in 1983, Pole Pole was euthanized in the zoo's elephant house. The next year, determined that her death would not be in vain, Virginia, Bill, and Will launched the organization that would become Born Free, which today works tirelessly to make sure each individual wild animal is treated with respect and campaigns to keep them where they belong — in the wild. It's an amazing story, and Born Free really is an incredible charity!*

bornfree.org

GLOSSARY

Aquatic
relating to water; watery things

Biodegradable
something that can break down naturally, without harming the environment

Bio-fuel
fuel that is made from something organic (like plants or animal waste)

Carbon dioxide
a gas made up of carbon and oxygen — plants need it to survive

Carbon footprint
this is how we measure the impact of our activities on the environment, e.g. through flying, traveling by car, heating, food production, etc.

Chlorophyll
the substance in plants that allows them to absorb light (it's also what makes them green!); it makes photosynthesis possible

Climate change
the change in the Earth's temperature over time; these are not normal or expected changes and can be damaging to the environment, such as global warming

Conservation
trying to preserve something natural; for example: an animal species, a plant species, a habitat

Decomposition
rotting (yuck); how dead things break down

Deforestation
when people destroy forests, cutting down trees and not planting any new ones; this often happens when people need trees for wood

Ecosystems
a group of plants and animals living together in a particular area; e.g. coral reefs, rivers, forests, etc.

Equator
an imaginary line that goes horizontally around the middle of the Earth, halfway between the North and South poles

Extinction
when a species of animals no longer exists; when no member of that species is still alive (like the dinosaurs . . . or the dodos)

Food chain / Foodweb
a chain showing which species eat which other species (or plants); it shows us how living things are connected

Global warming
the rise in the average temperature of the Earth's surface

Goldilocks Zone
the area around a star (like the sun) where the temperature is just right (which is why it's called the Goldilocks Zone!) so that liquid water, and therefore life, can exist on a planet; also known as a Habitable Zone

Greenhouse gas
these are the gases responsible for global warming, including carbon dioxide

Habitat
the area where a particular kind of animal or plant lives; e.g. a cactus's habitat is the desert

Habitable Zone
see Goldilocks Zone

Interspecies dependency
how different animals and plants depend on each other to survive (think *The Lion King* and the circle of life); this can be for things like food, protection, or shelter

Landfill
a big hole in the land where garbage is dumped and buried

Malnutrition
a health problem where an animal isn't getting the right food or nutrients in its diet

Microbeads
tiny pieces of plastic, often found in things like shampoo and toothpaste

Microscopic
something really, really small; you need a microscope to see it

Non-Governmental Organization (NGO)
totally awesome groups of people who try to make the world a better place

Oxygen
the gas that animals and plants need to surviiiiiive; we breathe it in with every breath

Phytoplankton (nano/macro)
microscopic plant-like organisms that live in watery environments; they help to feed pretty much all life forms in our oceans and rivers

Photosynthesis
how plants make their own food from sunlight, and fart out oxygen in the process; they do this by using carbon dioxide, water, sunlight, and chlorophyll

Pollinators
an animal that moves pollen from a male flower to a female flower, meaning they can create new flowers! Rad. Bees are an awesome example of pollinators

Pollution
adding harmful substances to the environment

Prosthetic limb
an artificial limb, which is often made of plastic, used to replace a missing body part

Recycling
reusing materials so that they can be made into something else

Single-celled organisms
a living thing that is made up of just one cell — how cool is that?

Single-use plastic
plastic items that are used once and then thrown away or recycled

Species
a group of animals, plants or other living things that all have similar characteristics

Sustainability / Sustainable management
taking an action that does not damage or destroy the environment

Synthetic
something that is not natural and is made artificially

Toxins
a poisonous substance that can cause damage

Water-borne diseases
diseases that are carried from one living thing to another through water

Zooplankton
microscopic animals that live in the ocean

ABOUT THE AUTHOR

Dougie Poynter is a musician, songwriter, designer, and author. He is passionate about the natural world and a keen conservationist, working with charities such as WWF, Greenpeace, and 5 Gyres. He is committed to cleaning up the planet and was instrumental in the campaign to ban microplastics in the UK.

ACKNOWLEDGMENTS

The wonderful team at Macmillan Children's Books — special thanks to Gaby Morgan, Cate Augustin, Emma Young, Mike Scott, Janene Spencer, Rachel Vale, Laura Carter, Sarah Clarke, Amber Ivatt, and the amazing Kat McKenna. To my agent Stephanie Thwaites at Curtis Brown. My manager Alex Weston at Riverman Management for literally picking me up off of the floor. My family: Mum, Jazz, and Paul. Thanks to the most fascinating and beautiful creature I know: Maddy, I love you.

To all the incredible contributors to this book. My heartfelt thanks to Adam Lowry, Amanda Keetley, Anna Cummins, Marcus Eriksen, Blue Ollis, Dara McAnulty, Edwin Broni-Mensah, Emily Penn, James Robson, Andy Bool, Jonathon Porritt, Josh White, Ariel Booker, Perry Alexander Fielding, Kate Arnell, Lauren St John, Lyndsey Dodds, Dr. Lucy Woodall, and Will Travers. The Gate, Richmond. Everybody at WWF, Lucy Parrat, Kehinde Brown. The Born Free Foundation. My band McFly — Harry, Danny, and Tom for being the beating heart of everything and for being my family. And to anyone else who has supported me in anyway, I appreciate it in more ways than I can put down in words.